CRAZY WORLD!
CRAZY WORLD!!

Someday It Will All Make Sense...Jayne Maria

Bert...my ex-husband

S...my oldest son

J...my youngest son

You must understand that I was born believing everyone spoke the truth and being very naive and gullible. Some people took advantage of that and I learned to be less vulnerable in time. My life has been an adventure in one way or another as you will find out.

I was due on St. Patrick's Day but gave Mom a couple false alarms before being born during a snow storm on March 21st. A nun asked my older brother what his mother had for a baby and he said a "false alarm" ...made the nun laugh and laugh. When my kids found out years later that I was born in what is now a home for special kids, they laughed and laughed.

Mom told me that when I was two or three years old she caught me eating a half of a worm in the sandbox. I couldn't have been conscious of this at that age because I still can't touch worms and don't even eat gummies in the shape of worms.

When it was time to go to kindergarten I refused to go until I got a cat. I never got a spanking and I can't recall how many days I missed but Mom found out about some kittens on Stony

Point road and we went out and I picked out a darling little kitten that came running up to me. She was a little female and I named her Sasserfrass and called her Sassy. She was with me for most of my school years. She was my comfort at times of stress and loneliness. I did go to school and had a fabulous kindergarten teacher...we made butter and read books and I loved that my teacher's fingernail polish always matched her outfits... she was a class act.

By the time I was in 1st grade Mom had to start working so she could help finance the older siblings through college. I used to sit on the vacuum sweeper to get Mom's attention because she was so busy all the time. I was the only child that didn't go to the Catholic school because there was no one to car pool with in the neighborhood. My Catholic friends later told me I was better off cuz there was a nun there that started a cult and alot of kids had bad experiences with that. I didn't mind Lincoln Stink'n (ha) at all...great teachers and classmates. I met Tessie and her Dad and my Mom car pooled us to CCD every Saturday. I hated missing Scooby Doo but oh well. We have some stories to tell about that Sister Ursula that was wicked and looked like she had jawbreakers in the mouth and was skinny as a rail. We were glad we only had to deal with her on Saturdays ...you can tell she was forced to be a nun and hated it. Tessie's Dad was the Principal of an elementary school in town and Sr. Ursala even gave Tessie a hard time that her Dad worked for the public schools. Tessie and I have enough dumb stories and adventures over the years to write a book. Like the time Tessie (as I always called her...short for Teresa) was crying that she had broke a drinking glass. Well it ended up being an olive jar that when empty could be used as a drinking glass. So we walked down to the neighborhood grocery store and bought another jar. BUT we felt we had to eat all the green olives....dumb shits...we could have dumped them in the garbage. It's a wonder we could ever eat any green olives again. HAHA!! It was always something or other with Tess and me like the time we got chased home from grade school by the Tripp kid and a couple guys. Of course it was winter with snow on the ground and we had full bladders so we ran and screamed and laughed and ran right into the ground and of course wet our pants. Tessie only had to walk down the alley and was home...I had four blocks to go with saggy wet underwear under my clothes...ugh

When I was in second grade and preparing for 1st Communion I had to go to confession. Alot of people complained of this but I always looked at it as a 'free shrink'. I remember coming out of church after confessing lying to my sister etc. :) and telling Mom that I felt like a chalkboard that had just been wiped clean. She laughed. My nun's name was Sr. Pierre and when Mom asked me what her name was I said Sr. Pee Pee Pee Sky.... the neighbor lady and Mom laughed and laughed. In 4th grade I was told by the teacher that "I was a nice girl but I had to stop talking so much". In fifth grade I got sick of my sister calling me 'Fatso' and ate my Mom's diet Ayd caramels...wait for it.

I remember Tessie's little brothers being born and her older brother Mike was like my brother but good even though he called us his little "pukes"! ha I heard years later that he had said if he ever had a daughter he would want her to be like me. I thought that was a pretty good compliment. Tessie's family became my second family ... I have met the best people through them and their mother Elaine became a very close friend to me.

My parents were the most unconditional loving people ever but they were busy with their lives and having more freedom since my siblings didn't go to college for long and I had so much fun with my parents when I got to be with them and their friends on a fishing trip adventures or dinner dates. They also played golf and were really good at it. My Dad would say to Mom "I'll clean the basement if you cook" and they'd have a party. I would take after them in later years as I was always entertaining, fixing meals and having parties.

I didn't have a conscience until I was in third grade. I used to walk part way home with a friend and a couple times I insulted her and made her cry. I still feel bad about it. I analyzed this to be a result of being insulted at home by older siblings. Her mother called Mom and told her I made her girl cry and when Mom confronted me about it I denied it. I also stopped doing it and I believe I started having feelings for others after that.

I would go out to my Auntie Marie and Uncle Ed's farm and stay for at least a week each summer. Auntie Marie was my Grma Loye's (Mom's Mom) older sister. They had one baby girl that was a "blue baby" and died shortly after birth. It hurt them so much they never had more children. Uncle Ed was crafty and would make toys for the children in the orphanage in Waverly, IA and Auntie Marie took me under her wing like I was her granddaughter and taught me how to bake and keep house etc. Uncle Ed would drive fast and right up the middle of the gravel roads going over a hill. I always thought we were gonna die. I would help her do wash with the old ringer type washer and she would "scrub my head"...her term for washing my hair. Mom and Auntie Marie would go out and cut the heads off of chickens and clean them. It never failed that one would get away and run right towards me. Hence comes the term 'running like a chicken with it's head chopped off'. I would scream bloody murder and run away from it until it would collapse on the ground. Who needed the "Outer Limits" ?! Then they would have us pluck the feathers off of them after they were dipped in boiling water and sometimes their claw feet would flinch. Ouuu Then they would go into Auntie Marie's basement where she had a sink and gut them and clean them. I remember hearing them say things like 'this one has alot of rocks in its gizzard or stomach or whatever." Ouuuu I would rather become a vegetarian than do that!! It is quite amazing that I even eat chicken today.

I helped them with chores and cherished every minute on the farm. I hated collecting eggs...those dang chickens alway looked like they were gonna peck you. I especially loved their Cocker Spaniel dog named Skeeter. He and I would hang out and walk down to the creek and I loved it. I felt free out there. Auntie Marie kept an immaculate house. She had style and good taste. I was always amazed when she would let me bring a baby chick into the house because it might doo doo and one did one time. She was tall and always said the Howard girls were noted for their long legs. She was proud of that. One time she needed some entertainment for her Pythian group which her Mother had helped start in town and she was involved in it. It was an Hawaiian theme. I was supposed to wear a grass skirt with a lei and dance to some Hawaiian music with a peony in my hair. I was only 6 or 7 years old and practiced constantly. I practiced so much that I sat up in bed one night and was dancing it in my sleep. I loved my great aunt but was embarassed by her some-times. When we would go into a restaurant she would tap her coffee cup with a spoon if she needed more coffee. She never worked as a waitress so didn't understand that was annoying and she never left a tip. She liked green stamps and bought alot of things with those. I ended up getting her china and have loved using it for holidays and special occasions. Grma Loye and Auntie Marie had the same pattern. I felt she was always critical of my weight. Through my fourth and fifth grade years she would comment that I was too heavy and I got sick of it but I loved her just the same. That probably contributed to me eating Mom's Ayd diet caramels later in 5th grade. She had a big heart and was good at everything she did. She crocheted table cloths and bedspreads and embroidered dish towels and seat cushions. I would sleep in their upstairs bedroom when I was there and I remember the sheets would be so cold that I would have to thrust around real fast in them to warm them up. I loved those days. They had an apple tree and we would pick them and make an apple pie. The big weeping willow tree had an owl in it and we would sit under it and eat watermelon. Her cookie jar smelled like black walnuts but I never really adapted to the taste of those. She had a large garden and we would pick strawberries and make jams and jellies. She is the only person I know that thought all china was made in China and pronounced Arkansas 'ar.kan.sas'. She thought she was a millionaire when they sold their eighty acres back in the '70s. God bless her sweet soul.

The family that lived across the road from my great aunt and uncle's farm were from Czechoslovakia and the kids became like cousins to me and Auntie Marie and Uncle Ed were like grandparents to those kids. The boys would bring horses over for me to ride. They had some tragedies in their family. The father would tell stories of being at a concentration camp. The father died young dancing with his wife at a party and the oldest boy and only girl died prematurely. There are still three boys living. I think so much of the ones who are still here...there will always be a connection. They said Uncle Ed and Auntie Marie were like grandparents to them. They bought Uncle Ed's eighty acre farm when they moved to town. I got a door off of the barn when they tore it down and made a table out of it. My Uncle Ed was so soft spoken and kind. One Christmas Eve he and my other great Uncle Morrie had a little too much to drink. As they were leaving Uncle Ed said "See ya tomorrie Morrow". We laughed about that for years.

One day after I was divorced I thought about that acreage that Auntie Marie lived on and wondered if I could rent it. Bear (my dog at the time) and I drove out to go see it and I couldn't believe it when I pulled into the driveway. That beautiful house had been torn down and the area was used for equipment storage and such. I got a big lump in my throat but that was happening alot those days.

When I was in fifth grade a horrible tornado struck my town. It had been the grade school's track meet on May 15th, 1968. It was an abnormally hot day. After school I was at my 4H leader's house to learn the parts of the sewing machine. I found myself in their basement with them while they were crying and holding their little dogs and glass and debris was crumbling down their stairs. My leader's husband got me home around downed trees. My home had not been destroyed. We were without water for awhile and the weather was rainy and cold. Thirteen people were killed and many injured. It was a very trying time in our lives. May 15th was the last day of school that year...God bless the ones we lost.

Christmas Eves were memorable when I was younger because all my awesome great aunts and uncles and grandmothers were alive and there was so much food and homemade goodies it was fabulous. Dad would get home from delivering mail around 3 or 4 pm and clean up and put on his Christmas tie and Mom would have some great food cooking and put on her Christmas shirt and the fun would begin. I never heard my parents complain about feeling tired or anything. They had as much fun as we did. My awesome great Aunt Verla would be playing Twister with us and she was well into her seventies. She was an artist and sang in a band and played Dolly in a play. She laughed alot and was a great person and cook. She would go to Arizona in the winter and Mom and Dad would oftentimes drive her down and stay for a few weeks. Mom loved to pick fresh lemons off the trees and Dad loved the pool. She never had kids and was Grma Loye's oldest sister... she made things special for us. She loved purple and one day when she was visiting in town I took her a bouquet of lilacs. She practically screamed with joy. She later had a massive heart attack and passed away that day. Aunt Verla was a great role model...she lived life to the fullest and laughed alot and loved life. She never had children and was widowed but made us feel like her grandchildren. She made everything special and made everyone feel special. The Good Lord spared her going to a nursing home or going through Hospice...He simply took her fast.

Aunt Maxine was Grma Loye's youngest sister. She was widowed and never had children and would have us for a weekend

and treat us to a movie and dinner and usually do our fingernails by soaking our fingernails in Palmolive soap first. I usually
paired up with my cousin from Cedar Rapids to go to her house.
She took us to Sound of Music at the theater. I rode the bus
down to Waterloo and when she got me off the bus I had gotten
carsick and had vomit all over me. She never said a word and
took me into the bathroom and cleaned me up and we went on
to the movies and out to eat. She was a classy lady and we all
loved her very much.

Mom and Dad would have Santa come to the house at Christmas time. I always asked for a horse and Dad always said I
would get horse droppings. One year Santa wasn't able to come
so they staged it that there would be a huge box of gifts on
the front porch and someone would be outside to ring Santa
sleigh bells and I believed it. That was mystical and magical and
effective!! They would yell "Santa just left!!" We would get to
wear something new to Midnight mass and Dad always had to
carry me out to the car afterwards because I would fall asleep.
We relaxed on Christmas Day and that was Dad's only day off
before he went back to work. I could be alittle shit. One year I
probably was 10 years old when no one was home I took each
one of my gifts in to the bathroom and unwrapped them and
wrapped them up again. I knew everything I was getting and it
ruined my Christmas...I would never do that again. As for the
Easter bunny I stopped believing in him when I saw my oldest
brother's big square teeth had taken a bite out of the carrot I
had left for him one year when I was in 2nd or 3rd grade... figured the Tooth Fairy was a scam by then. HAHA

When I was in second grade I had my tonsils removed. I had chronic ear infection and this solved it. I remember being in the hospital the night before and the nurse came in to give me a shot. I tensed up my butt as tight as I could and I felt that shot go through my body and hurt so bad. I was such a dumb shit to do that ...I guess I always lived and learned. Uncle M (Dad's brother) who was still the "rich uncle" sent me a clear glass snowman full of candy. He was always so thoughtful in everyway and I still remember that. We had that snowman container for years. Uncle M was the one who was watching me one New Year's Eve when Mom and Dad went out and bought shrimp coctail. He wanted to introduce me to it and I didn't want to disappoint him so I tried it. I was probably in lower grade school years and I put it in my mouth and went directly into the toilet and spit it out. I didn't tell him but it took me years later and I was finally able to eat it.

When I was in seventh grade I went with a sweet guy and would walk me to classes but we never kissed or even held hands... we were both so shy. That guy could write the best love letters ever...he went on to marry a cute gal from high school and have five kids and they are still married...bet he still writes those love letters. :)

When I was old enough to stay alone on nights when Mom and Dad went out with their friends they would usually order me a small Opal Special pizza and Dad would look at it like he wanted a piece but didn't want to ruin his appetite. Opal Special were Italian sausage, green olive and mushroom and our favorite toppings. I remember Leo Greco and the Pioneers playing on TV while they got ready. When they left I would put music

on and lip sync to Dionne Warwick and Engelbert Humper-
dinck and choreograph dance moves to them. I loved having
my own variety shows and I was into entertaining. The only
mistake I made was doing a somersault on Mom and Dad's bed
and breaking the foot crossbar on their four poster bed. We got
it glued and it was ok for many more years. I remember Mom
and Dad coming home and laying in bed reminiscing the night
and laughing so hard. I thought 'I want to be like that when I
get older'.

When I was in 6th grade I discovered Mom's Ayd diet caramels
in the refrigerator. She apparently wasn't using them so I read
the directions and ate them with some warm water. I lost my
appetite and went from 92 pounds to 72 pounds. I looked like
a walking stick...they worked and I loved it. The school nurse
sent home a note about my weight loss but I never showed it to
Mom and I don't know if she ever knew I ate them. She probably thought it was a growth spurt. I wish they still made them.

As an adult I used to organize little variety shows with my
nieces and nephews on vacation with family and I got active in
the local community theatre bunch called Stony Point Players. I
performed the Sally Field role in Steel Magnolias in 1994 and it
was a smash hit. I performed as Sister Robert Anne in Nunsense
and became president of the group in 1996. I fundraised and
helped the committee purchase the art deco Charles Theatre
for $120,000. I organized golf outing fundraisers and directed
many variety shows and dinner shows to raise that money. I
loved the variety shows...we had such a fun bunch of people. We
had dance acts, comedy acts, singers and we gave money to the
Salvation Army. We honored the military and even had my Dad

and his honor squad performing the posting of colors. It was fabulous. In 2000 we performed the first play in the theatre. It was Dracula.... I played the role of BuBu Padoop and it was the most fun I had ever had in my life. Some of the staff were the older guys who had started the theatre bunch. We laughed and had a blast. I left for the airlines after that. I did help my friend direct Nunsense Amen in 2008 at the Charles Theatre...it was a huge success and had men playing the roles of the nuns...same dialogue as Nunsense.

Back when I was in 7th grade I had some friends that had horses and kept them out on a farm and my folks were friends with the owners. Mom and Dad thought it might be a good way to keep me out of trouble and I was always working at the pool and had money. It was up to me to pay for all the expenses such as rent, food, vet etc. I took care of things and got an Appaloosa from some people that needed a two year old mare broke so she could be ridden. Her name was Dolly and man was she ornery. If the other horses & riders were taking off, she wanted to go too. She caught me offguard one day and she reared up to take off when I wasn't expecting her too and my left boot got stuck in the stirrups. I went off her and next thing I knew I saw hooves and was being drug along the crushed gravel driveway. Fortunately I didn't get kicked in the head and I came loose from being dragged. I had gravel stuck all over in my back. My friends helped get me cleaned up and I never told my parents. I remember the agony of taking showers while my back healed. I thought for sure that Mom & Dad would get rid of Dolly cuz they were already going through enough with my brothers being in Vietnam at the same time and both getting wounded. I truly learned to pray hard during that time. I worried about the stress it put on my parents...there was no Skype or anything like that...just prayer and faith that they would return safely. My Dad would sit on the front porch and look at the sky and worry about them. He was a worrier and Mom was the prayerer. Needless to say... Dolly was sent back to Orchard IA to breed in the fall. The next spring I got a two year old gelding to break and I got to name him Shay Kismo. I fell in love with him. He was my horse and he didn't like anyone else to ride him. He tried to scrape my brother off on a building and my sister had a sore neck from getting thown off him. I spent all my time outside of work with him. We went on trail rides, sleepovers in the barn and I gave him baths in the creek. Come fall I was ready to buy him and he was for sale so Mom and Dad bought him for $200 but there again I had to pay all rent and expenses. I was the only girl out there that went out to ride my horse on a regular basis. I lived and breathed the farm with Shay. Of course we had some wild times with our sleepovers. We would play the "blanket" trick....always looking for the most vulnerable newbie to trick. We'd put a blanket over the victim and keep asking for an article of clothing until they would say "I don't have anything else on" and then we would yell "THE BLANKET!!!" haha!! We'd all been through it but then the victim would have to go out in the yard and oink around the scrub three times or howl at the noon naked, do a cartwheel or something funny and gross.

It was during these years that I met my Junior High bestie Jayne V. We couldn't believe our names were spelled the same (Our Dad's liked Jayne Mansfield) and our Dad's went by the name of Dale (even though my Dad was really Francis Dale). My Dad said to Mom when I was born that "if we are gonna name her Jayne ...we are gonna spell it like Jayne Mansfield. My family pronounced my name 'jay.ne' all my life. 'JV' had gone to the Catholic school...she had two older sisters and her Dad had a junk yard on the edge of town. I was walking carrying a bunch of paints on a tray in 7th grade and I dropped them being the klutz that I am...some old bag of a teacher was yelling at me. JV came running up to help me and we were friends from then on. JV's Mom had a whole drawer of cigarettes so she would never miss one pack if we wanted to try them. We rode our little stingray bikes up around the bend off the gravel road going to the farm where we kept our horses and lit up. I inhaled and almost coughed myself to death. I turned blue. It was decided smoking was not a good idea at that time. I think that was our 9th grade summer. We could drive cars around in the maze of the junkyards and JV told how she would find money and diamond rings etc. in some of the junk cars. Her Dad kept his boat in a stripped out school bus... I thought that was cool and clever.

A friend of mine had a bunch of us out to her farm house in 9th grade for her birthday and I believe this was my first encounter with alcohol. I can't recall what we were drinking but I think it was whiskey. We ate, drank and were merry. Some guys came out and were hitting on us and I told them off. I still can't believe that the next day I went home and crawled into bed at 9:30 a.m. and had a hangover and Mom never found out.

My 9th grade year was another milestone year because my oldest brother and his family came to live with us for several months. My brother's hootch had gotten blown up in DaNang Vietnam where he was stationed with the Marines and he worked on helicopters. CH-47s were the kind he worked on with two routers. He was wounded and sent to Okinawa to recuperate.

That is where he met his future wife. They lived together for a while and got married. She had been married to an alcoholic and divorced. She had two little boys from that husband. Those two little boys were to become the most important men in my life. Woody moved them in with us in the summer of 1972 and it was the most fun time of my life. My folks became grandparents for the first time at young ages and they were smitten. Achan was going to start kindergarten in the fall and Ken was three years old. I bonded with them and them with us. I took them to ballgames and the DQ and swimming and everything I did. They were like the little brothers that I wish I would have had. Mom and Dad set up my bedroom in the basement and one time Ken was messing in my room and broke a ceraminic Snoopy that an aunt had made me. He looked at me and felt so bad and tears came into his eyes. I could have cared less about the Snoopy statue... I didn't want this little guy to get upset about it. They would shower with their mother in the basement and then Ken would always get away from his mother and run upstairs bare naked and try to make his armpits squeak ...it was hilarious. My folk's 350 pound friend Harvey would put Ken up on his shoulder and Ken would say "Big Harbey"...it was so adorable. Achan was quieter and smart. He taught me how to spell and say some words in Okinawan. One fall day Dad called Mom at work and said that my sister-in-law had opened up all the windows and had the heat on. She would teach us how to make some great Asian food and we all loved stir fry the best. Achan dressed up like a Pittsburgh Steeler and Ken a bum for Halloween. It was the first time that they ever trick or treated. Achan liked school and visited his kindergarten teacher every summer he came back. While Achan liked the song "Billy Don't Be a Hero" I introduced him to "I Shot The Sheriff" and all the great 70's music I listened to. He still goes to concerts where the Doobie Brothers etc. are playing. My friends loved my nephews as much as I did. People still ask me how they are doing after all these years. I would take them out to see my horse and there wasn't much that we didn't do together and I fell totally in love with them. Then came the day that they found a place for them to relocate. It was Camp Lejeune, Jacksonville, NC my brother thought it would be similar to Okinawa in that it was close to the ocean for seafood and climatewise the same. The day that they left Mom and I cried and cried. It tore our hearts out to know we wouldn't see them as much as we had. Every time they came home or we went out to visit I bawled my eyes out to say goodbye. Our bond never broke. They grew up to be the most faithful wonderful young men imaginable. Achan became an engineer and Ken an physical therapist. They have been with me through thick and thin and much more like family than I could ever imagine.

Sometimes when we had a sleepover at the farm we would invite others so Tessie got invited alot. One night she decided to scam me with her imitation of a bum. She put a nylon over her face that really camouflaged her good. She was chasing me around the farmyard ...me in my Daisy Duke jean shorts and cowboy boots and all the girls were screaming. When I got across the picnic table and took a good look at her... I couldn't tell it was Tess at all...was convinced it was a bum and he had done something with Tessie. I felt responsible since it was my night to entertain friends and I ran down to the stable and grabbed a set of reins and hid out thinking I would whack him when he came downstairs. Thank God one of girls clued me in that it was Tessie or I could have badly hurt her or worse.

One night just Tessie and I spent the night out at the farm alone. Her boyfriend and his friend came out to visit. Tessie ended up in the haymow making out for a while with her boyfriend and I stood outside with the other guy asking him why he wanted to kiss me...ha...He ended up saying "well I kiss my sister!" yeah well he wasn't gonna kiss me...poor guy... my hard-to-get days.

I have so many stories with Tessie and her family that it is hard to write them all but another one that sticks out in my mind involved me getting car sick. Tessie asked JV and I to go shopping with her Dad and little brothers. We were in seventh grade and stopped at McDonalds in a town 30 miles away to eat before coming home. One of Tessie's brothers was showing his food while he was talking and that sort of started it. I was notorious at getting sick especially if I didn't sit up front. I was sitting in the back and thank God by the right door. I started to get an upset stomach and I knew I was going to vomit. I rolled down the window and we were going seventy miles per hour. I remember JV holding my head out the window as I puked and the wind blowing it back into my hair. Tessie said I was gasping for air. Tessie's Dad kept looking back as he was driving and making sounds like "OH!!" "Oh my!!" Perhaps it was making him feel a bit sick too. I don't remember if Tessie's little brothers said anything cuz I was oblivious to anything but the gut wrenching thing I had going on. Next thing I remember we were parked in front of my house and my long brown hair on the right side of my head was stiff and standing up. When I walked in the house Mom was there and knew exactly what had happened. Tessie later said that I never got any vomit in the car...amazing.
One day JV and I were riding our horses along the highway and JV and her horse had crossed the highway to the otherside.

Along came a big Winnebago and the stupid driver laid on his horn (NEVER DO THAT) and the next thing I knew Shay and I were behind JV and her horse on the otherside. By rights we should have been smashed to smithereens. JV and I got off our horses and our legs were shaking like rubber bands...was that Divine Intervention or what??!!

I was notorious at getting carsick if I didn't sit up front and it was like getting over a hangover to recuperate. Mom tried to give me a dramamine before we left on a trip and that helped. It's amazing that I was able to fly as much as I did in the future... but fortunately I didn't get airsick.

I spent alot of time with my Dad's Mom because she was in town and alone. Grma G. was common as dirt. She wore cobbler aprons and liked to bake pies, caramel rolls, cookies and jellyrolls etc. She was the first one to turn me on to the Special K treats... also known as Scotcheroos if made with Rice Krispies. She also had a huge garden till the year before she died. She was into game shows so we watched alot of Password with Allen Ludden, What's My Line and To Tell The Truth. I watched all the Watergate hearings with her. She was widowed longer than she was married. My Grpa G. died of his third heart attack at the Post Office in 1959 at the age of 51. My Dad was with him. Grma thought the world of us grandkids. I got to decorate her artificial Christmas tree every year and put silver icicles on it. She had worked at the tractor plant in town in the foundry. It was said that she worked as hard as the men carrying heavy things. She didn't believe in 'strikes.' She never drove so think of the money she saved not having a car. She and Grpa had built a cool house on 5th Avenue with hardwood floors and a fireplace. It was close to town so Grma could walk with her little grocery cart down to get groceries. When I was little she had a little mean dog named Brownie that was always trying to bite me. I remember her putting a fireplace screen up to keep him out of my bedroom when I stayed the night. One night he was scratching at it until he knocked it down and next thing he was up on my bed. I loved animals so it baffled me that he was so agressive towards me. I think he was jealous. He had gotten shakened by a big Great Dane when he was younger and it made him mean. I used to pick Grma up for church and one time when I dropped her off I was standing outside the car and a bird pooped all over me ...I hope it was the bluebird of happiness. I remember that was one of the most disgusting things that ever happened to me. Grma wasn't into fashion or decorating... I got that from my other Grma. Grma G. had both her hips replaced when she was in her seventies at the Mayo Clinic in Rochester, MN. She had a cardiac arrest between the hip replacement and her hysterectomy but survived. She lived a good life after she had gone through all of that. My Dad was sold on the Mayo Clinic after going through that with Grma. I used to daydream while looking at the Assisi Heights Spirituality Center. It made me think about being a nun. There was winding road leading up to it and I looked at it out of the waiting room window of the Methodist Hospital where Grma G. was having her hip replacement. Dad and his brother were the best sons to their Mother that anyone could ever have. Dad would experience the Mayo Clinic later in his life.

Grma and Grpa Loye were awesome. Grpa farmed the family homestead founded by his parents when they came over from County Kerry area of Ireland. Grpa Loye's dad had dark red hair with a beard and mustache. Grpa's mom gave birth to three boys that died weeks apart of Tuberculosis in the millhouse in the late 1800s. Great Grma Loye had four more children after that. The youngest one was my Grpa Loye. Poor Great Grma Loye threw herself down a cistern and died in 1931…there was definitely depression on that side of the family. Grpa had a really sweet sister. He also had a brother and sister who were nasty. His nasty older brother never talked to Grpa and had a sweet wife who got Alzheimers. This brother married into money and farmed by my Grpa but never offered to help Grpa in any way. They never had kids. I went to their house with Mom one time when I was five years old and I got the worse vibes from him. He ended up hanging himself in his garage and leaving over $40,000 to our Catholic church. That was like over $100,000 in the sixties. Grpa's nasty sister wanted my Mom and her sisters to become nuns. She was an old maid herself. When my Mom and her sister were old enough to go to high school they had to live in the upstairs of her house so they would be in town. One time she threw out some flowers my uncle-to-be had sent to my aunt. Their neighbor Harvey picked them up off the street and gave them to my aunt. Harvey would become an important part of my life in years to come. Grpa's health started to fail him enough that in 1953 he sold the farm. He didn't want to sell it but had to. They moved to Cedar Rapids IA where his cousin lived. Mom kept the bill of sales from the farm. She really wanted to buy it. Grpa had three girls and their husbands had careers of their own and were not interested in farming at the time.

Grma Loye had style. She had great taste in decorating and in fashion. Their barn roof two story house in Cedar Rapids

CRAZY WORLD! CRAZY WORLD!! ◆ 21

was beautiful. Grpa worked as a produce manager at a Me Too Store and always brought us the best fruit and vegetables when they came to visit. Grma worked at Collins Radio which is now called Rockwell International. Grma decorated her diningroom in a celery color wallpaper and had a chandelier and beautiful cane back diningroom set and china closet. There were french doors to their bedroom and coming into their living room area from the entry way. They rented the upstairs out. Their yard was huge and limestone landscaped. We had so much fun with Easter egg hunts. One year Mom's two other sister's families and all the 11 grandkids dressed up for an elegant Easter dinner. It was fabulous. The girls had patent leather shoes, dresses and bonnets and the guys wore suits. There was 19 of us and we had a fabulous Easter egg hunt after we ate a delicious ham dinner. It always seemed to be nice warm weather for Easter in Cedar Rapids. It was always certainly memoriable.

There was an old mansion across the street from Grma & Grpa Loye's house. It was abandoned at one time and my cousins and I went over and looked around. There was also a cemetary across the side street from the mansion and we would go in there and look into mausoleums and freak ourselves out. My cousins were always like family to me in that we were close in age and we always had fun together.

Dad took us to the Minnesota State fair one year and we saw John Davidson and The Carpenters. Dad was stroking out leaving with his new Chevy and the bottle neck traffic. We then went to the Minnesota lake with my folks and their friends and we took a pontoon out and we were fishing. Out of nowhere came a storm and we didn't think we were gonna make it back to shore and neither did the resort owner. Even the Lutherans were praying the rosary with us. Harvey was my folk's realtor friend who was close to 400 pounds and even with his weight back there the back was coming out of the water. The lake was so rough. We made it but it was one of the scariest times I ever remember being out on a lake. When my Grpa Loye passed away I made a comment to Harvey that I didn't have a grandpa anymore and wondered if he'd be my grandpa. He took it seriously and taught me how to fish and treated me awesome and always made me laugh. He even talked to me before I married Bert and told me that "I'd never be rich". I should have heeded his word. He looked out for me and even though he has passed on I will always have a spot in my heart for him.

On a High School Art Club trip we went to the Wisconsin Dells. We took lime vodka and all sorts of beverages to imbibe. I drank too much lime vodka and I can tell you that I will never drink it again. JV put a pine cone up to Tessie's head and the sap got in her hair. She was crying and her hair was all waded up. JV said "Pine cones are edible" ...that did not help the situation. We camped out and didn't get much sleep and I don't remember much about the trip but we had fun and drank too much... I never had a tolerance for liquor and was always glad about that but suffered hangovers because of it.

When I was in High School it was the years 1972-1975 and post Vietnam era. We all looked like leftover wanna be hippies. We wore the same bellbottom jeans and a different top everyday. The guys and gals looked the same ...we had long hair parted mostly in the middle. There weren't manicures and pedicures yet and we were very cheap to maintain. I always worked so I never asked for money. I started working in 7th grade for 60 cents an hour as a basket checker at the pool. I practically lived out there and rode my bike 3 miles one way to get there and back. Tessie was out there with me. We met some cool people who were senior to us that lifeguarded. One of them was a wrestler who went on to coach college and Olympic wrestlers as well. His brother who we called Boogaloo was a close friend of mine. Boog's older brother Mike told me all about Dan Gable...a wrestler and a coach and the University of Iowa who he idolized. He told me how Dan's sister had been murdered and how that made Dan excel in his competited skill. It was a story that I never forgot and through my Uncle Jersey who was at the University of Iowa at the time...Mom, Dad and I got to meet Dan and watch Chris Taylor wrestle. Chris was a heavy weight wrestler...unbelievable...google him...he is deceased. I also found it amazing that in later life I came to know the best friend of Dan's sister that was murdered. I heard that story all over again with more sad details. What a small world.

Dad let me drive two girlfriends Jayne and Jane up to a Todd Rundgren concert in Rochester, MN. I was just 16 years old. We were getting hustled by some guys and one of them asked our names and we said " Jayne, Jayne and Jane" They said " Oh yeah and we are Bob, Bob and Bob". We thought that the funniest thing...we also found it bizarre that Todd Rundgren looked like he had a banana in his leggings!!

When it came to conversing with each other among my friends in the 70s we greeted each other with "Fu*k you". I mean the F word was prominent and used all the time. I frankly can't stand the word to this day but use 'F it' in intense times. I never seemed to get away with anything. One time an older gent pulled out in front of me in his car and I 'flipped him the finger'. Of course one of Dad's Postal buddies saw it and told Dad....I had to hear a little lecture on that. But what I am not proud of is the fact that I spoke using the F word during that era but when you hang around with people who say it every other word, you tend to do it too even if you don't realize it. Well one day a good looking friend of the Big D (my high school steady) and who I should have been going out with instead of the Big D pulled me aside and said "Jayne you are such a pretty girl but it just doesn't sound good hearing that come out of your mouth". It cured me.

I went to a party with my boyfriend. It was at a place in town where some shady characters lived. One of the guys that lived there ended up being put in prison in 1974 for murder. This guy was a handsome man but had psychological problems. He had gotten kicked out of the service for beating up a drill sergeant. He came up to me and gave me the biggest kiss on the lips and he was just trying to urck my boyfriend and the others who were far too scared to say a thing to him for doing that. This guy would see me riding my bike home from the pool and he would be riding on the back of tractor and he would grab my ram horn handlebars and pull me along behind him just to see if he could freak me out. It did but I never let on that it did. He was accused of stabbing a nurse to death in her upstairs apartment so hard that it broke the bed in two. Wow...to think I was kissed by someone who could do that to someone. I always wondered who lived below the woman that got murdered and I later became friends and neighbor with that lady who lived below.

There were many adventures and good times with my high school friends and those horses...but when I graduated from High School and was going to go to college I had to sell Shay. It happened fast and I can still see his big eyes looking at me from the horse trailer as it rolled out of the farm's driveway. Mom and Dad got their money back for the horse but I have never gotten over Shay leaving my life. I still can't stand to think about it...tears at my heart. I never knew what happened to him but in hindsight I should have kept him and gone to school at a community college and not three hours away at IOWA.

My family took Minnesota lake vacations in the summer. We had a lot of fun in cabins and eating fish that we caught and playing cards especially Huckly Buck at night. When I was in Junior High years my folk's friends Dorothy and Harvey (realtor in town) and Ernie and Gerry (beauticians in town) got Mom and Dad going to this resort up by Spicer, MN. We went there for almost 40 years. The owners were friends with us and they built a pool in the side of the hill...it was so nice. We have alot of fun memories from there. My Dad's brother kept a camper there and went up there alot from Marshall MN. I got to take JV up there one summer. The owner's son was cute and he introduced us to smoking pot. Unlike Bill Clinton I did inhale. We got the munchies after that. I ate four slices of peanut butter toast and 3 or 4 ice cream bars. The Big D was upset I hadn't tried it for the first time with him. Oh my gosh I wasn't into pot but it was a fun experience. There was a rope on one side of the lake and we would swing out from that and drop into the lake. We would rent pontoons and spend most of the day out there... so fun. I loved it up there ...I didn't really care if I ever went any where else.

When I was in Junior and Senior High school we didn't have drama yet but we had variety shows called Juhiva (Junior High Variety) and Damuco (Dance Music and Comedy). I was always involved in dancing and comedy skits. They were a great time!!

I went to a Doobie Brothers concert in Davenport with five other high school classmates. Dad called them the " Grubby Brothers ". We camped out along the Mississippi River and I got introduced to malt liquor. I was running to the porta-potty and ran right into the ground. I remember seeing a bright light coming down the river...it was a barge! It was a fun weekend with three guys and two other girls and no Big D.

My Dad was amazing. Dad went to work at the Post Office when he got home from World World II. His Dad had been a rural mail carrier and even delivered with horses back then. Dad went to school at a small business college but decided he didn't want all the complaints of the Post Master so never pursued it. He actually enjoyed getting out and walking his route and the 10+ miles he walked daily. He rescued an old lady who had fallen off her porch in the dead of winter once. It ended up this lady was a millionaire and an alcoholic. There are alot of stories he could tell about people when you are a mail carrier and walk the same route for 34 years. He didn't complain about his job as a mail carrier even when it was beastly cold. He would just call Mom and tell her to have a hot bath drawn for him. He never said he parked cars and raised the flag for high school home football games ...he just did it and received a plaque for doing it for 50 years!! One time when I was a cheerleader I was able to run over to him and give him a kiss when he was taking the flag down. He was a faithful Legion member and helped with

Bingo and putting flags out for Veterans Day etc. and earned a lifetime membership. He was on the honor guard squad and fired guns at funerals and in parks honoring deceased veterans. He never complained about it...he just did it with the greatest respect. It was reported that one time a funeral procession was passing Dad on his mail route and he stopped and removed his hat and bowed his head. That was Dad...always respectful. He was also reliable and dependable. He would show up for coffee at his Mom's the same time every day. Grma could count on him for anything and Grma would complain to him about everything. Maybe that's why he didn't complain. Ha! Dad and his brother were the greatest most considerate and caring sons to their Mother that I had ever seen. The way that children should be to their parents.

Dad's brother M was awesome. Unlike my Dad he enjoyed cooking and touring and could build anything. He married late in life and up until then he was noted as our 'rich uncle'. I remember him having a Chrysler that had engraved plate by ashtray that said it was made for him. Uncle M lived with Grma G for years while he traveled around to dealerships for the tractor factory in town. He married a woman who was a nurse. She couldn't have children because she had cancer when she was younger and the radiation had destroyed that option for her. They ended up adopting a baby girl and later adopted a little girl from Korea. One time while up at the lake my aunt and we decided to stop at an octopus ride and go on it with my little cousin who was probably three years old at the time. My aunt oftentimes wore a wig well....that wig couldn't handle the spinning around and went flying off. My little cousin was freaked out looking at her Mom with bobby pins all over her head and my aunt and I were laughing so hard we could hardly stand it. Then we heard the old man operator below say "Oh myyyyyy!" It was lucky that wig didn't fall into the gears of the ride. That was one of the hardest that I ever laughed. My aunt and uncle also provided such a tranquil atmosphere for us when we visited and we enjoyed doing it often. My uncle added on to a beautiful house that overlooked the St. Criox River and the Mississippi River in Prescott WI. The boys and I went skiing at Afton Alps near there and would spend the weekend. I always had a special bond with this aunt and uncle and when they got older they would winter in Naples, FL. One time my uncle asked me if I would come down and drive their new Nissan Altima home for them. I asked a friend of mine who had a flexible schedule to go with me and she said she would. We flew into Ft. Meyers FL and drove down to Naples. We stayed several days and when they were ready we took them to the airport. We had decided to go home via New Orleans since we hadn't been there yet and it was the Music Festival going on in April and May. My friend was bragging about not getting a speeding ticket in years and she was going 90 mph when a patrolman up around the Gains-ville FL pulled us over. They are rednecks in that area and she could not talk herself out of that ticket come hell or high water. I think it cost her $295. Ouch

When we got to New Orleans we stayed at an older five star hotel. It had a balcony right on Bourbon Street. I had to go down to the coffee shop to get wifi which I thought was sort of weird. I found that it was hard to sleep in this room because the garbage truck and the street cleaners come by early. A poolside room would have been quieter. Live and learn. We went to the Cat's Meow where they serve 3 to 1 drinks and tanked up there and karoaked. I can't remember what we sang but I couldn't get out of my choir sounding voice on a rock and roll song and it was quite hilarious. Then we ventured down Bourbon Street and every bar had a fantastic musical group...whatever they played, they sounded just like it. For example one place was playing Michael Jackson music and vocalist sounded just like him. I was digging this and had never experienced anything like it. I loved the atmosphere and all the beads and boas. It was awesome!! After a few days we ventured on home and ran into some ter-ranial rains the closer we got to home. We made it safely and without any more speeding tickets.

I chose the University of Iowa to go to because I was pursuing nursing and it was an hour away from where my high school boyfriend went in the Quad Cities. I got a $500 March of Dimes scholarship. I started going with the Big D when I was 15. He almost stalked me...he was everywhere I was...he showed up at the farm, he was at the pool, watching me in classrooms at school, he pursued me everyway he could. I now was a check-er at a local grocery store. I was a cheerleader and involved in many clubs at school. He was the starting Quarterback, great bball player, baseball player...BMOC (Big Man On Campus). When his family first came to town I thought he was the best looking man I had ever seen so it didn't take me much to get smitten. But my advice to all you teenagers out there...don't go with anyone at this young age for this long...you miss out on too many other things in high school and it's too young to be that serious. The Big D had a full ride scholarship to play bball at Augustana in Rock Island IL and he was a year older than me. I had fun at Iowa and enjoyed the football and basketball games and my uncle was an assistant athletic director under Bump

Elliott so he was keeping a protective eye on me. I spent alot of time down in the Quad Cities with the Big D but realized I needed to find out if I really could handle being a nurse and it would have been my third year at Iowa before I would have done any student nursing so I transferred to Moline Pubic Nursing School which no longer exists but I was in the Quad Cities and didn't have to travel as much. I found out that being a student nurse was tough. I had to deal with people that were dying of cancer. One lady had most of her brain removed and I had to take her rectal temperature... it normally runs around 99.5 and her temp was like 94 and their was feces all over the thermometer and she was dying. It was sad and tough...I hadn't dealt with death much except my maternal grandpa when I was in 10th grade. My other grandpa had died when I was 2 years old so I don't remember that. On day when Dad came out to the farm to pick me up, I told my Dad that I had thought about Grpa that day. Dad said it was his Dad's birthday...I never knew that. Isn't it funny how things like that can happen??!! I go to a Hawkeye game with my alumni friends every year and every year I think in hindsight that I wish I would have broken up with the Big D and stayed at Iowa and switched to an Art major.

I lost two very important men in my life my summer after my freshman year at Iowa. I now lived in an apartment in Rock Island, IL. Mom called and told me that their best friend Bill had died of a heart attack at the Post Office. He was only forty-nine. Bill was a clerk at the Post Office and was telling everyone how he had won the City golf tournament over the weekend and fell over backwards. Dad was a mail carrier and was with Bill as he was with his Dad when his Dad died of his third heart attack at the Post Office. My poor Dad was in shock

and walked over to the bank's drive-through where Mom was
working and told Mom. They had to go tell Bill's wife Vonnie.
Not only were Bill and Vonnie best friends with my folks but
their folks were best friends with each other. This was a couple
who had stood up with each other when they got married. They
danced at the Terp in Austin, MN or the Surf in Clear Lake,
IA every weekend. Mom and Vonnie's waists were these tiny
little things. Our families vacationed on Minnesota lakes together and were so close. Bill and Vonnie's kids are still close
with me and came to see Mom and called her. One lives in New
Mexico and one in Dyersville, IA. My parents were Godparents
to their daughter. I sat out on my front steps and bawled my
eyes out. My high school art teacher had dropped dead of a
heart attack at his Lake Okoboji store. I loved that man too...he
was so much fun and I had many treasured memories with him.
I couldn't believe I would never see those two men again.

I had fallen away from going to church when I left for college
but I didn't turn away from God. I could miss school easier than
I could miss church when I lived at home and guess I burned
out alittle. I never desired to change from the Catholic faith. I
loved honoring the Holy Trinity, the Virgin Mary, the Angels
and Saints, the palms, holy water and incense and everything
that went along with it. I do believe it was built on the rock and
foundation to never change and like Fr P would say "It made
sense." I do feel that there would not be a shortage of priests if
they would allow women to be priests and if priests could marry.
I also remember Fr P saying that he wouldn't want to come
home to a 'honey do list' if he worked all day being a priest.
HA... true. Those years were the worse years for me. I needed
the Lord in my life and I needed the Eucharist...I was stronger

with Him in my life and the good Lord knows I would need Him for years to come. I also had resented the Lord for causing my ex-husband Bert to have Muscular Dystrophy' and his father for dying so young. I have learned never to do that again. God is all good. I will praise Him and thank Him everyday for the rest of my life. I will never know how people get through life without Christ and I never want to find out.

The Big D and our life together was crazy...I was staying with him in a big old house with other Augustana guys and German shepard dogs all over the place. Lots of drinking, smoking pot and partying going on all the time if you wanted it. We watched Monty Python together on Saturday nights. I remember going out to a bar where they were serving 3 for 1 drinks and I don't know how many Jack Daniels and Cokes I had but when the van pulled into the driveway, the door slid open and my head fell out and I was sicker than the devil. I felt like the almighty geyser...still have not drank Jack since. I was too stupid not to quit even when there were several drinks in front of me. We went to awesome concerts like the outdoor one at Haythorn Race track in Chicago that featured Lynyrd Skynyrd, Eagles, Gary Wright, Peter Frampton, Marshall Tucker, Yes and more. They had built bridges over the race track and people would 'mooo' as we crossed them in herds. HA! The Big D loved the Yes band and I ended up painting every album cover of Yes for him. I guess future girlfiends of his hated them and wanted him to get rid of them but he didn't...haha. The Red Cross tents were set up and I remember thinking how stupid these people were to be all drugged up so bad that they would miss the concert. I also got to see George Carlin in Davenport and he was so funny... died too young too. I also saw David Bowie in Chicago and he was awesome. We had alot of fun but as the drugs got more involved, the drama got intense and I had to escape it ...my life was going nowhere. I was around alot of drugs but wasn't into them...but I was too stupid that I didn't think that I could get busted with them and luckily that never happened. I was hoping it was a phase that would pass in the Big D's life but it didn't pass during my time with him.

I got in a car accident that broke my pubic bone (hair line fracture). A sixteen year old ran a red light and t-boned me in my little Volkwagon bug ...when it rolled I strattled the gearshift and that caused my pubic bone to fracture. I was in bedrest for a long time and weighed 98 lbs when I got out of the hospital. I hated the food and only ate the dairy...like JV said to me "Don't you think God was telling you something?" Oh yes I believe he was telling me to go home. By 1978 I had lived with the Big D for a couple of years ...I didn't want to be a nurse and the Big D was involved with some things that I couldn't approve of so I left him after 6 years and went home. I started going to church again. I made a big mistake during this relationship.. I loved The Big D more than I loved myself... so I felt lost without him and I got depressed. The Big D was a narcissist and I just couldn't see it... love is truly blind. I needed to get my head on straight again. I wish the Big D would never have come into my life. I had actually considered becoming a nun before I met him.

One incident that happened while I was still living in the Quad Cities and that still remains a mystery to me is this. I worked at the largest liquor store in the Midwest when I was with the Big D and got along good with everyone. It was good money and I liked it. I bartended and it was a college bar so weekends were super busy. The manager of the liquor store decided he would pull a prank on me for some reason. He had me pose in a bikini on a ladder and I was supposed to be in a commercial for some type of liquor. He airbrushed my bikini off and painted in what he thought my private areas looked like to make it look like I was naked. I don't know why he would do such a thing but it really hurt me. I wasn't a vixen or anything of the sort. The Big D went crazy on this... he wrecked some things in the bar after a Christmas party and the boss ended up giving me a $1000 for the incident. I threatened the jerk that did this that I would tell his wife and he begged me not to. I oftentimes wonder if this picture is still circulating out there...thank God this was in 1977 and before wifi and Facebook. So damn strange that people can do these things to others for no reason. I was Ms. Naive and Gullible.

Dad knew that I missed the Big D's German Shepards and got me an Irish Setter pup that was born on his mail route. I named her Cessna and called her Cessy. She was one of a large litter and we got to take her home at 3 weeks and she fit in our hand. We bottle fed her sweetened condensed milk and she howled at night so I put a music box in her pen. She grew into a beautiful loving dog who shared many a memory with my family. A magician friend of mine said she was a "magic" dog because she was born on Halloween. She slept in the boy's room once they came along until the night before she passed. She lived to be 13 years old and there was not a dry eye the day she died... especially Dad. She had cross country skiied and walked and swam and everything with him. She loved to eat sweet corn on the cob with or without butter. She sat at the bow of Dad's Jon boat when he took it up river...a remarkable best friend was she.

When I got home from the Quad Cities I didn't know what to do... I didn't want to start another career right away cuz I was depressed with my life and was very frustrated. My depression took me to a level of running away and I wanted to leave life but I didn't know how to do it. I spent one night out at Tobacco Road in my car ...tried to gas myself... a wild turkey startled me and ran by me. I don't know why but it made me realize nature is so precious. The next night I got a hotel room in a little town 18 miles from my hometown and thought I could figure out something else probably pills. All this time my poor parents were losing their minds with worry looking for me and I never even considered that...I thought everyone would be better off without me. The police found me and Dad asked me if I wanted to get some help in town or away. I chose to go out of town and my older Italian psychiatrist worked with me for a couple years and it was determined that I was not bipolar ...just the depressed side showed and never a manic side. This doctor and his wife were like family to me and even had me up to their house in Decorah when I was hospitalized up there initially. He got me regulated on some meds and I never got depressed again...I was able to tolerate the ups and downs of life without spiralling down.

I went on a blind date set up by my couple friends and met Bert ...we were in our own little bubble and I thought he was so calm, easy to talk to and smart. I had ridden horses with his sister but I never really knew him until now. He played guitar and had been in a band with one of my neighbor friends. He was three years older than me and had graduated with a Business degree from the University of Iowa. He played the guitar and liked to dance and we had so much fun. We never lived together because it was sort of taboo to do that in the 1970s and we had our parents and grandparents in town and we didn't want to embarass them. It would have been better if we would have lived together cuz a month after we got married I could tell that Bert drank alot and spent alot on beer and cigarettes a month. But we were married and it was only 6 months after I had broke up with my six year relationship and it was a rebound. Thank you Fr. P for telling me that years later. I didn't realize till years later that my Mom and Dad weren't happy about me marrying Bert. We were married for 5 years before S came along. I was afraid to be a Mom but absolutely fell in love with my little snugglebug. I nursed him and loved being a Mom so much I decided to do daycare in my home so I wouldn't have to leave him. My Dad was so thrilled to have a grandchild in town that he came over every day before he played golf and held him so I could run errands or whatever..they totally bonded. Jordan came along a couple years later and was so precious...always smiling and laughing. I had my Huck Finn and Tom Sawyer...my boys were so cute in their jean cutoffs and suntanned torsos and bare feet. I loved having them along for everything.

When I worked in an insurance office and managed the Country Club pool...it was like their own private pool with pool birthday parties and all sorts of fun. We brought a salamander home one night from cleaning out the pool but ended up taking it back out cuz we read that they can dry up and we didn't want that to happen. As the boys got older, we would pack up the car with a cooler full of sandwiches and chips and go to the Airport Lake for the whole day from 10 a.m. to 4 or 5 p.m. The boys took friends and they would float on the lake, fish and swim and play in the sand for hours. S and J were definitely outdoor kids.

One year I had an old convertible that had holes in the canvas top and when it rained, it rained on people in the car. I also feared that I would be driving in a Flintstone car and the floor board would rust through. We had fun in that car though. We just buckled up, rolled the windows up, put the so-called roof down and took off. Great memories were made in those crazy lazy days of summer.

While we were doing all this...Bert was pulling away from us. He had fallen down a section of basement stairs and pulled a bunch of groin and stomach muscles. As the years went by, he walked worse and worse... people were asking me all the time "What's the matter with Bert?" I was so sick of telling him to go to the doctor and I could hardly stand him. I figured he needed back surgery or something. One night we were arguing about it like we always did and I decided to go talk to our local priest about it. Bert was so mad at me for doing that and it was bartered that he would go get his back checked if I would go get help. Bert went to the Mayo Clinic in Rochester, MN and he was diagnosed with Muscular Dystrophy. I went to Five East and led group sessions because there wasn't anything wrong with me except this all was very depressing. I felt bad that Bert was alone at Mayo but he was so ornery about it and had me sent away from my kids...there was always drama in our lives. If I had it to do over I would have divorced him then in 1987 but everyone would have said it was because he got Muscular Dystrophy and not the real reason...he was an alcoholic! Bert and I had been married one month and I saw what he spent on beer and cigarettes and went to talk to his grandmother who I adored. She said he was young and should be slowing down. I hung in there.. I really didn't believe in divorce. It would be hard for me to leave him financially too being that I didn't have a degree in anything...but Bert made very little at his third generation Hardware store.

Fr. P was a new priest in town. He had come to town and he had been close friends in mentoring a man from town who was going to become a priest. That man had died of cancer so Fr P came to town to be by this man's mother. Fr. P had an interesting past in the fact that he was raised Episcopal but lived in an area of Des Moines where there were alot of Catholic families and he oftentimes went to church with them. The Episcopal church was the English version of the Roman Catholic Church but their priests could marry and be women. I knew this because Bert was raised Episcopal. Fr. P had one sibling and he was "special". His parents were older and his father had been very strict. Fr P had cancer when he was younger and he bartered with God that if he became a priest would God let him live to spread God's word ? It was granted. I loved his homilies... he was a great speaker. Bert joined the church so we were blessed with his teachings. I was able to sing in choir during those years and attended as many funerals as I could because I was having trouble understanding and getting a handle on death and figured his homilies would resolve that. They did but I remember gasping when he addressed two young children who had lost their father. He represented Jesus perfectly at that moment.

Fr P wanted to do something dramatic for the Christmas season to hang from the bell tower. I told him about the cheesecloth ghosts I saw for Halloween and this object had to be light...only a certain weight could hang from it. He said that would work. We got together and made a big cheesecloth angel and named her Muriel. We had so much fun creating her and it was fun hanging around in the social hall and hearing the other older priest call for Fr P and Fr P would say "Don't answer him right now... he can come find me and get some exercise"...ha... priest are so human too. We got Muriel done and most comments were really good. Of course I had one person say that "she was weird". Why do people say negative things like that? Is it to put you down or what? If I don't care about something I keep my mouth shut and certainly don't express it to the creator. Ugh. Muriel hung for many years with little touch ups each year. She was stored in a parishioner's barn and stayed good for years. I remember Fr P was constantly burning himself with the hot gun gun...those hurt like hell. Fr P was at our parish for 12 years...he was an influential priest. I sensed that from the beginning. When Fr P left in 1991 I made him a sketching of Muriel and put a fancy frame on it. He loved it. I was hoping that he would still be here for S's first communion the next year but that wasn't meant to be. Alot of things were going on in the world and I valued his opinion on it. He was a special man. I sensed that from the beginning. He was relocated to Dyersville IA where some of our close friends moved to. We got to see him when we went to visit our friends. They were so lucky to get to continue hearing his homilies. After Dyersville he was relocated to Gilbertville IA near Waterloo. I ran into him in a store in Waterloo looking for sheets one day and I also ran into him in Chicago O'Hare airport and got to visit with him a bit. He felt so bad about Bert's drinking and our divorce. Bert had joined the church and Fr P was a big part of that process. When Fr P developed cancer again in his later years I was one of the people he requested prayers from and he would keep updated about his prognosis. I was so honored to receive letters from him with follow up news about his journey. He was 10 years older than me. He stated that he apologized to anyone he may have offended. I didn't go to his funeral because I knew it would be huge and thought they could use the seat that I would take. I was also flying at the airlines and it could be such a pain to get off for funerals at times. I regret that because it was "Fr P unique" of course and at the Basilica of St. Francis Xavier in Dyersville, IA. He was buried in Dyerville too. God bless Fr P forever...wonder what he would say about this world today. After he passed away, I received a call from a priest friend of his. He said that he had something for me from Fr. P. He said that he had gone through Fr P's things with him prior to his death. They came across the framed sketching of Muriel that I had made Fr P for his going away gift. Fr P had said " I believe this young woman might like this back." Mom rode with me over to Garner IA to get it and I watercolored this priest a picture of "Hand it over to God" painting that I had given many for gifts. It was amazing that Muriel had come full circle.

Fr L was a priest at our parish during Fr P's reign. I was a representative to the Parish Council from St. Anthony's Circle and got invited to cookouts and such. On one of these occassions it was held in the patio of the Rectory. Fr L was mixing me Black Velvet and Cokes and the big bunch of parishoners were imbibing, laughing and eating. I hadn't figured out that my limit was two yet and I have no idea how many I drank but I ended up like the great geiser again and throwing up in the night. I layed in bed most of the next day with the shades pulled...ugh I really did not enjoy throwing up that much but seemed to never learn my lesson. I didn't drink very often but when I did I didn't seem to know my limits...yet. This was during the era when I worked at American Family Insurance and managing the Country Club pool. Summers were busy but fun for the kids and me. I remember drinking up to 8 Canadian Clubs and waters at a Country Club outing. That is when I realized that could not continue. Alcoholism didn't run in my family (Praise God) and I wasn't going to start it. Fr L golfed alot and I got a membership included in my being the manager. Fr L and I got to be friends...like he was a brother who was a year older than me. He officiated at my paternal grandmother's funeral that was just before Christmas and gave a wonderful eulogy that she was "going home for Christmas". Fr L was Irish and he made me laugh... he was a good egg in my book. I've always heard you should never defame a priest but I can honestly say I only remember having some awesome priests at our parish. If there were any bad ones, I was too young to remember them. Even if I knew of any I was told that you should never defame a priest afterall they represent Jesus.

I started to give communion to shut-ins. I really enjoyed taking the Eucharist to people who couldn't get out to church. I had one couple that I had trouble with because the stench was so bad in their home. I would get out to my car and gag. All I could think is how can this be that I am blest to be giving to shut ins and I can't do it?! I mentioned this to a friend and she said to put some Vicks under my nose so I would smell that instead. It worked! I also gave to an elderly lady that never got out of bed. I had to dissolve the host so she could swallow it. Of all the shut-ins she was the one who made the greatest impact on me. She had the most fierce cat that I have ever seen in my life with the biggest fangs. It almost looked cartoonic because it didn't look real...I brought cat treats every time I went there.

I thought of all the things I would do in between giving her communion and all she could do was just lay there all the time. She was so sweet and never complained. God bless her. It made me think "I should never complain."

I started having bat problems in my attic of my bungalow on 3rd Avenue. I was washing some whites in the basement one day and I went to put them in the dryer and I saw what I thought was a black sock. I picked it out and instantly realized it was a bat. I HAD WASHED A BAT!!! I flew up the steps taking six steps at a time and bellied out in the kitchen with my arm and fingers tingling from the touch. Of course the boys were parading the neighborhood kids through to see the bat Mom had washed. I was in my back bedroom one night and two bats were dive bombing me in bed. Everytime I would raise up they would take another dive at me...it was like being in a horror movie. I got a guy called "Batman" to come solve the problem. Praise the Lord.

Back in High School Tessie and I would get in these moods to have alittle slow gin. Tessie worked at the Charles Theatre and Drive-in Theater and came to know the owners and operators. These women were fun loving gals who would let us come out to the College Apartments and have a drinky poo once in awhile even though we were only high schoolers. The legal age was 18 years old which was coming up pretty fast. Well on this night we were drinking slow gin and stopped by their place. Next thing we knew there was a knock on the door and it was our local young good-looking priest...who was also referred to as Fr. What-a-waste. Tessie and I about 'shit' cuz we thought we would be in trouble....here we were sitting there with red lips

CRAZY WORLD! CRAZY WORLD!! ◆ 43

and half snockered. But he was cool and the girls had an 'obsene' Christmas tree and there were fake boobs hanging on it and he contributed something to it too....I will leave it as that....hahaha

I organized fundraisers every year for Muscular Dystophy that correlated with the Labor Day Jerry Lewis Telethon. Bert even got an award for being a good example to our elderly neighbor to use a cane and we were on television down in Waterloo during the telethon. Bert had a problem with having this disease and his issues about his father seeing him with it etc. I begged him to talk to Fr. P who he knew from having joined the Catholic Church a year prior. He never would talk to anyone and then his father died at the early age of 57 and Bert sunk into a terrible state of mind...his drinking escalated. There was always a dramatic fall or accident and there was never any money. Bert broke his leg and had to have a rod put in it and another time he fell outside and cut his face up so bad he needed stitches. He was always drunk while all these thing happened too. He smelled so bad from drinking that I couldn't stand to be around him. The vodka sweat out of his pores. I slept on the daveno couch at night... the boys saw it but I didn't tell them anything...I should have. I just wanted to spare them. But they heard us quarrel and I'm sure that upset them. Another tip to people facing these problems...always tell your kids what is going on so they don't misinterpret things the wrong way. I believe it would have made a big difference in future years had I done this.

In 1993 I decided to go back to school to get my Associate of Applied Science degree in Drafting and in 1995 graduated. I and a 19 year old man were the only ones graduating in two years at that time... it was such a hard study. I even helped the

19 year old with the final math problem because I figured it out first. My mind was good with math back then. KIMT-TV did an article on me being an nontraditional (older) student going back to school. It was one of the hardest things I've ever done. I had to take Calculas and Physics for some of my classes. I graduated twenty years after I graduated from high school. It was to be a stepping stone to take some graphic marketing classes but I never got to that point. At one point I didn't think I would get all my assignments done and I flopped back on my bed and started to cry. It was my young sons that came in and said "You can do it Mama" that got me through it. God bless their precious hearts.

I was into fundraisers of many kinds during these times when I lived in town. I got to know alot of people by doing Jazzercise at the YMCA and two gals asked me to be on the committee for Bone Marrow Awareness way back in the 80's. We were successful at getting alot of people signed up to be donors and one of the committee members was a survivor thanks to Bone Marrow Transplant. Her story is a miraculous one to me. She told me in utter detail everything that she went through as she will always remain my "HERO" as she is thriving today.

It was January of 1999 and I had planned a meal for my Mom's birthday. Bert had been going to the office where he was now the Floyd County Auditor on the weekend to supposedly work. I called to tell him that the dinner was ready and he should come home and he couldn't even talk. He was completely intoxicated and come to find out that he had switched from drinking beer to drinking vodka because supposedly you can't smell it. Oh yes you can!! Especially at the rate he was drinking it. Why was I always so unsuspective?? I guess I was raised in a home without any alcoholics and drama. I was just floored at the realization that he was drinking so excessively and drinking vodka. One noon hour my insurance agent called and told me that our van's insurance was cancelled cuz Bert hadn't paid it. He was home for lunch and I confronted him and he started to cry. He hadn't been paying any bills and he was in charge. I had to take the interest money on his life insurance to catch up. It was a total nighmare. I always tell my young friends that no matter how much you love your spouse...always keep your finger in the finances .. I hated to pay bills so I neglected checking on them till now. Yes I liked to spend money and rang up the credit cards at times but I always had something to show for my spending which is better than peeing it down the drain or puffing it up in smoke. There wouldn't have been Christmas or birthdays if I hadn't put it on cards cuz there was never money for anything. Christmas would not have happened if I hadn't used credit cards at times. When your husband spends over $500 of our modest income on his habits and addictions there isn't much left. Well I can't really recall when this happened but it wasn't long after Mom's birthday that Bert got caught drinking in his office and a deputy sheriff escorted him to a dry out facility and he had to go to save his job. It was such a relief to me because I had been trying to get him to get help for years and he punished me by sending to get help every time I would set up an intervention or anything. My good friend Georgie went to my folks and told them that they had to get me out of there because it was killing me. I was too proud to tell my parents and hated to admit to the havoc that we were living in. It was in my head that I had made my nest and I had to lay in it. Bert stopped his check from coming to me so I could pay bills and buy groceries and that's when I decided I was done. If he couldn't give me his check so I could feed our kids etc. then the hell with him...I was done. Get counseling for it while you are in rehab Bert and bye bye.

I guess rehab was really hard on Bert...he had to drive 30 miles every night to stay there and stay dry after he started back to work. He seemed to be doing pretty good for quite awhile. When the boys were in 8th and 10th grades I decided I needed a job with benefits...I had been working 60 hours a week without benefits at an Ostrich Ranch and my drafting jobs weren't working out cuz I was always at the bottom of the totem pole and got laid off. I really didn't like drafting, it was a stepping stone towards getting a graphic arts degree but that would take time and I didn't have time or money now. I went to my cousin's wedding in Texas and met a flight attendant from American Airlines and learned all about that career. I came home thinking the boys and I would move to Dallas and I would get an agent's job. Sean and Jordan were all upset about us moving ...they had girlfriends and didn't want to leave. I remember we were talking to Bert and he was yelling at the boys that they had to move and they were crying and I started crying and we got in a huttle on the floor and cried and I decided I wouldn't move them but if they supported me I would try for the flight attendant position. I asked the boys if they would support me if I got hired and they said yes. Of course I would be the one who would be gone. My Dad was really against me doing that cuz he hated to fly and would be worried about me. Well I went for an interview anyway and got hired!! March of 2001 I started a 6-1/2 week training in Dallas, TX. It would feel like 6-1/2 years. Bert was doing so much better that I asked him to stay with the boys while I was at training and he said he would. I thought this might be a good way for him to make up for lost time and make some good memories with the boys. Oh boy...it did not turn out that way. Being away from Sean and Jordan about killed me...I missed them so bad and felt like I was deserting them and I would cry my eyes out to my Mom on the phone at night. I had never been away from home for so long. I didn't know that it was a living hell back home. Bert had fallen off the wagon and started drinking and he was not getting out of bed for work... he was so frantic for alcohol that he would have S buy Listerine and he would drink it!! He also was not feeding the kids...he'd give them money for McDonalds and junk like that. All he did was lay in the bed in the back of the house and the boys would come and go as they pleased. J told me his Dad said he had the flu but J said he had the "bottle flu". Mom kicked Bert out of the house. One week before my graduation from 'nylons and high heel boot camp' I got a call from Bert...he told me I had to come home and he couldn't handle it anymore. I left class and went to the bathroom and projectile vomitted and went on back to my hotel room with a massive headache. I found out the next day that if that had been a FAA accredited class that I missed that I would have been sent home. You can never trust a drunk. YOU CAN NEVER TRUST A DRUNK. My parents became aware of what was going on and Mom called me and said that I had worked so hard and done so well that they would help with the kids so I could finish up my training and not to quit. I loved my kids so much there are no words but I felt quilty for what they went through. American Airlines approved four people to come down to my graduation so Mom and Dad brought S and J down and I cried so hard when I saw them that I thought I would die. Being gone that long was the hardest thing I had ever done up to this point. My folks are like saints to me and I never worried when they were in charge of things back home. They were my rock, stability and foundation in my life that has finally made me a strong and stable person. I am so glad that in their later years I was able help them in every way I possibly could and had stayed in town to do so.

The stress of my situation with this alcoholic spouse would tense up my back so bad that at times I would have to lay down in bed and suffer through it until my back relaxed again. I had such loathe for Bert that it wasn't until a devote Catholic friend gave me a prayer from a Marian conference that I got over it. You were to recite the prayer over and over again until you could truly mean it...I wish I still had that prayer but passed it on to someone else. It worked. By the time I could say it sincerely and meant it, I had forgiven Bert and didn't comdemn him anymore. That made things a whole lot easier to cope with.

Bert ended up drinking alcohol and not eating and had a stroke or alcoholic poisoning awhile later...I thought he was going to die... I bought the boys suits for his funeral and prepared myself. Funny that after all the chaos and trauma that emotions still take hold. I cried for two days just like a runny faucet at the thought of him dying. I guess all the good memories came flooding in and how things should have been. He will always be the father of my children and that was reason enough. He ended up in a nursing home at the age of 50 but he still continued to drink and smoke and asked me to stop coming to see him... he had someone who brought him liquor. I found out as long as he didn't act up and didn't have a doctor's order not to drink, he could drink. He got MRSA in his feet and to this day has lost both legs. I guess I can be a bleeding heart so it was better that way. In Bert's defense he tries to help the other residents at the home and has been a positive influence on them... God bless him for that. If I would come into alot of money, I would get him out of there and into his own home with people to help him. We have come full circle to where we can talk and be friends again. Forgiveness is very important.

I sang in the choir at my Catholic church and started being a cantor as well for over twenty years but couldn't do it after I started at the airlines because at first I was gone most weekends. I missed doing that. One day I was leaving church and it was winter so I was letting the car warm up. An older couple got into the car ahead of me and went to back up and banged right into my car. Then they went forward and put it in reverse and backed into my car again. It was like they were oblivious to me being parked there but a couple across the driveway saw it all and couldn't believe it. They banged and banged and banged my car before they finally drove off. I got out and looked and there was luckily no damage to my car but this other couple and I have laughed our butts off about this for years.

I taught Red Cross swimming lessons for twenty years at the city pool before going to the airlines. I also gave free adult lessons because I feel it is so important for everyone to swim and know how to properly wear a lifejacket because you can save yourself. I taught many adults some being the nuns at my parish and my dear sweet Mother who was deathly afraid of water. Dad was always the "fish" that took us swimming. One day Mom and Dad went out on the river to fish but it was really windy. They ended up coming and Mom got off on the dock and it was rocking so much that she fell in. She had her lifejacket on she knew to hold on to it across her chest and it brought her right back up!! On their way home Dad saw my car at a convenient store since I had just come home from a trip. He came in and said "Mom just fell in the river!!" There was a long line in the checkout lane that heard him and when I looked out the door, there she was sitting in Dad's pickup with a big smile on her face waving at me. Her red stocking hat was still on her head dripping wet. I couldn't help but laugh... Saints be praised!!

My career with the airlines was a very fulfilling one. I got through reserve and ended up with a dozen Someone Special certificates (complimentary cards for great service) so I could fly home every time I had a day off but it was gruelling and I really don't know how I made it though except by the grace of God and the fact that I had to in order to make money and have benefits. A passenger heard me telling another flight attendant that I needed some SOS passes to get home to see my kids on my days off and he was an AAdvantage member and surprised me by giving me a whole sheet of them. Hip Hip Hooray!! Dilemna solved!! That was also the flight that we heard strange sounds coming from an engine. I learned to sit on the jumpseat and say " It's normal" and smile even though I didn't know if it was.

Reserve was absolutely exhausting...I might fly seven legs in a day. (a leg is one segment from city to city). Sometimes you forgot if you were coming or going with that many legs. I would think "Did I say that announcement or not?" "Why are my tights twisted around my leg?" HA "Am I losing it??" If I had my own airlines, I would never work anyone that much. Your safety goes downhill. One night on a layover I woke up and went to the bathroom... I don't know why but I went to jump back into bed in the dark and landed on knees on the floor next to the bed... it's a wonder I didn't break something. I was flying with a really funny older Captain from Arkansas one time and I again was exhausted and got up to go to the bathroom during the night. This time I kinda threw myself back into bed in the dark (never turned on a light so I wouldn't wake up too much) and I hit the headboard with my face. I ended with a black eye. I tried to cover it up in the morning with makeup and my cheater glasses but the Captain saw it and said he hoped it was from "rough sex". HAHA

Raising my kids on 3rd Avenue was so much fun...the block overflowed with kids to play 'night games'. We were only two blocks from the Catholic grade school they attended and the families were so fabulous. We had block parties every summer where we would close off the block and grill out and let the kids run wild. Every May 1st or May basket day I would make up cups with popcorn, mints, nuts and chocolates and the boys would try to be the first to ring the neighbor's doorbells and leave the baskets and run off before the kids would see them. Halloween was always a blast with over 400 trick or treaters coming to our block because all the houses had their lights on.... some played spooky music and lots of us dressed up to greet them. There remained a bond with me and the 3rd Avenue families even after we moved away.

I remember waking up and the ice would be crackling on the limbs of the trees and it was pitch black out and I'd have to get up at 3:30 am to get ready and drive to one of the airports and fly into my base Chicago. Oh dear God...I have spun out in front of semis on the icy highways and got stuck in foot deep snow and almost everything you can imagine. One night at 1 a.m. a herd of deer were crossing in front of me and I pressed on the brakes and laid on the horn and started praying. I never hit one. My guardian angels were always there to save me. Maybe my praying the Divine Mercy on the way helped too. Of all my twenty some years as a commuting flight attendant and being in and out of hotels everynight on the road (some good and some bad) I can honestly say I never was afraid. I was always vigilant and smart and never walked alone at night or jogged around areas I did not know. I also always checked my hotel room thoroughly before locking myself in. The airlines had taught us to check behind thick drapes, under the bed and in closets as we entered our rooms...predators had been known to hide in these places and would assault and even kill flight attendants.

I met lifelong friends through airline training. We took turns crying and wanting to quit...we laugh about it today but at the time it was devastating and real. Vee was from Quatemala and made everyone laugh all the time with her big emerald eyes and sense of humor...she was a riot! She always said " my God!' and "Shut up!" when she thought someone was pulling her leg about something. She liked men and Latino music so was always fun to go to the bars with. Vee was a hairdresser and cut the music director's hair for our class song before graduation. I'll never forget how hard we laughed when the electric trimmer slipped in her hand and left a bald mark on the back of his head (of course the side the audience would see). She put black magic marker on it to cover it up.

They got us up early at training and kept us busy all day long and they were long days. If we felt we were going to fall asleep during class we would stand up. We had to be able to say the evacuation drills verbatim and open each exit correctly. We learned how to do CPR and use the AED machine to resucitate passengers. We learned how to act in emergency situations with fire extingushers and many devices. It was grueling but very informative and we had to go back to Dallas which was our headquarters to review and recertify every year. It took us two days to requalify. The instructors would come in and check us on our grooming being sure our makeup, uniforms and nails were all proper. It was unnerving at times but we got used to it. I still apply lipstick or lip gloss pn my lips every half hour and keep my nails flawless. Some classmates would get eliminated for having their cell phones on or dressing inappropriately...how ridiculous. To get that far and blow it for nothing.

Mary Kay was ten years older than me (I was 43 years old at the time) and she was a smart, classy and spunky-she was from San Francisco, a mother of two and had gotten badly hurt by her husband when he had an affair on her. She had been devoted to him and the business they owned and ran together and decided to break away and do something she had always wanted to do. She started at AA to eventually go to International which is what many wanted to do but we had to fly domestically (within US, Mexico, Canada and the Caribbean) for one year before we could proffer for it. I had come to training to give passengers "above and beyond service" as well as receive better wages and benefits and give my kids a chance to see some of the world with me.

Julie Murphy was a beautiful Irish blonde from Dallas and had a Texas accent. She was a true gemstone...she loved everyone and everyone loved her. She made everyone feel upbeat and important. She had her realtor's license so did that on the side. She did not cross over to the regionals after we got fuloughed the second time. She gave us a little Statue of Liberty to commemorate our flying in New York. Every time Mary Kay and I went to Dallas to requalify we contacted Julie and went out to dinner with her. Then all of a sudden we couldn't get a hold of her anymore and we thought she maybe didn't want to keep in touch with us anymore. It was awhile later that Mary Kay ran into someone who knew Julie and said that she had died of aneurysm and there were over a thousand people at her funeral. We cried that we hadn't found out. We couldn't believe that Julie had been taken from this Earth before her two boys could make her a grandma. But we could believe that the dear Lord wanted her in Heaven because of her precious happy and fun loving soul. God bless Julie Murphy forever.

I met people who will forever be in my life and we became an airline family ...a family away from home. They were from all over the world... Andre was my Phillipino friend from Honolulu who took me under his wing and became my airline son. Andre had lost his mother when he was only eleven days old and was so good to me. We were in a crash pad together with a bunch of other flight attendants in a hotel room in Chicago. Crash pad is what we called the hotel rooms we stayed in while we were out flying and did not cost much because so many people shared it...that was the only time we used the word "crash". It was not fun but necessary because it kept expenses down when I was out flying and already had expenses of a home and children back home. But if the weather was bad and lots of flights were cancelled, there could be more than 10 flight attendants staying in a one hotel room and that was never fun. People were getting up at all different times and no one rested too well but that was the way it was until you got past the point of needing to have a crash pad. I only flew six months before 9/11 happened. I was on reserve every other month and was on a scheduled month when it happened. I was home and heading to the bank drive through when I heard on the radio that is appeared a small plane had crashed into a trade center building. I got home in time to see the second one crash into the second tower. I was on my 10th day of eleven days off and had to sing at a funeral the next day and go back to work the day after that. The organist and I were so in shock of it all that we had a hard finding our music to practice for the funeral. When my boys came home from school they had been watching it all day. S came running in and gave me a big hug and said " I don't know what I would have done if you would have been on one of those planes" and to J it was all surreal. S said when the towers collapsed it made him so mad he was ready to go fight the terrorists...in a few years he would enlist in the Army and serve time in Iraq. I was very fortunate to not be on one of those American flights.

When it was time to go back to work...I had to drive into Chicago because nothing was flying yet. It was so eery and quiet as usually there were six flights in formation to land at a time. I got to my crashpad and hung out for a few days then a roommate and I decided to get in uniform and go over to the airport and find out what was going on. 9/11 happened on a Tuesday and it was Saturday before I flew for the first time. The flights were sparce and passengers would clap for us for showing up to fly. I thought "we aren't the heros... the victims were. I remember my male flight attendant saying that "just last week a passenger called me an SOB and now you can hear a pin drop." My first flight was to Phoenix. It was good to get 'in the saddle again'. I bought each of my crew small onyx crosses to commemorate our first flight after 9/11.

My first medical incident at American Airlines was going from Chicago to El Paso, TX. I was the #1 flight attendant and an older couple coming back from Poland were sitted at the bulk-head. The bulkhead was the first seats in a cabin without anyone sitting in front of them. The woman started to complain of chest pains and said her nitro was packed and in the cargo area. I called the Captain to inform him and he had me ask if there was a physican onboard. Thank goodness there was and he was able to obtain the medical kit with the nitroglycerin and put some under her tongue. I got her on the floor, elevated her legs and put a cool washcloth on her forehead. She had broke out into a sweat. We landed in El Paso and the paramedics come on and got her off before anyone else deplaned. Her husband had dementia and was no help on any details or information. As far as I know she recovered.

Several times we had to carry a deceased soldier onboard our aircraft...that was a very solemn time to see the widow leaning over the casket to say goodbye...rarely a dry eye and the whole plane seemed to give respect and sympathy to the situation. A flight attendant died in her hotel room in Italy and we had to bring her home...I just prayed I didn't die that way.

One trip I had a Captain in NY that was wearing a turban and when he spoke English with his arabic sounding tongue I thought the passengers were gonna stroke out. It was too soon after 9/11 and I was told it wasn't the Middle Eastern people who wore turbans that you had to fear...it was the ones that didn't wear them. How can you tell? I have to tell you I felt sorry for the innocent ones because they were suspected too. Like the Japanese after Pearl Harbor. A flight attendant and I got in a taxi late one after a trip and it was a cab driver in NY who wore a turban and didn't appear to speak English. I thought we were dead being American Airlines flight attendants of all things. He obviously understood English and got us back to our crashpads but oh the anxiety. The lady that lived below our crashpad taught English to Middle Eastern people. She said they liked what they could get for free from our country but said they hated America. She said they all disappeared two weeks prior to 9/11. Hmmm

Another tense time was when I was catching a bus at 1:30 am from JFK International to my place in Queens. I had a driver who looked like Stevie Wonder and I was the only one on the bus. Every now and then he would say something and I thought it was to me. He seemed to be talking to himself and it was scaring me. Finally he looked back at me and pointed to his left ear which I couldn't see had a ear bud in it. He was on his phone to someone... Praise the Lord!! I told him I thought he was crazy when he got off the phone and I was never going to see my family again. We started laughing about it.

Some of my friends and I went to the one year anniversary memorial of 9/11 in New York. We were advised not to go to the big one with President Bush because security was high so we went to the airline's memorial. Members of the victim's family carried large pictures of the deceased around, they let doves fly and played the bagpipes. I met surviving firemen. It was a day much like the weather it was on 9/11 and we all cried. I'll never forget it. LET US NEVER FORGET!!

Another hairy experience in NY was when I had to commute to Newark NJ airport from Kew Gardens in Queens super early on a holiday. One of my roommates went to the subway with me at 4:30 am and I got on and when I got off I discovered that the bus that should take me to Newark was running less due to the holiday and I had to take a cab which costs me $50. I cried and paid it and got there on time. UGH!

One of the best things I learned from a Dallas senior Mama (which is what we called flight attendants with higher seniority) is that 1.) Welcome each passenger with a smile as they board. 2.) Never give them attitude. Best advice ever. Whenever I worked with a flight attendant that gave attitude to her passengers, she received it back tenfold. I never had to have anyone removed from the plane and feel very thankful for that.

There were rumors that the airlines would be furloughing again which means to lay off with the option of being called back again. Sure enough by October I was furloughed and went home for six months. I couldn't afford Cobra healthcare insurance so went without it and worked two jobs under the table and one job over the table to make ends meet. I was home with my boys but it was stressful financially. While I was home I adopted a rescue dog who was half chow and half black lab...she looked like a little bear cub and thus that became her name "Bear".

We already had a rescue cat that S had brought home from the Ostrich ranch. Killer as J had named her was lifeless when S brought her home. She had been abused at the ranch and was starving. She had tried to eat a part of a red rubber ball. I held her and bawled my eyes out because I had seen her at the ranch and didn't want to feed another mouth since I was going through a divorce. She was meowing at me so dramatically I had to tear myself away from her and then when Sean brought her home in that shape, I felt so quilty I haven't brought her home two weeks sooner. We took her out to the vet and he got the rubber ball out and pumped her full of electrolytes and told us to hold her with a warm hot water bottle all night and see what happens. When Killer woke up she looked like she had died and gone to Heaven. She made it !! She was the best cat ever even though she was mentally off alittle, she always scratched on the fireplace bricks and not the furniture. She did not like having Bear in the house initially. One time when Bear was sleeping Killer came out by her and hissed at least a dozen times. HAHA I loved the cat/dog combo and they became good buds in the long run. I remember waking up and Bear would be on one side of me and Killer laying down my spine on the other side like a heating pad and I thought "life doesn't get any better than this."

By April my class was called back and we were sent to New York LaGuardia for our base. I was hesitate about it being that is where 9/11 took place. But I knew I had to do it and seven women and I found a place in Kew Gardens, NY and started our new commuting life. My commute was two legs now. One leg through Chicago and then the second leg to New York LaGuardia. One time with bad weather it took me eleven hours to get back to New York. Commuting was always a worry as we flew "standby" which meant we were last to get on and only if there were open seats but it did not cost us. We paid $2400 a month for an unfurnished second floor of a three story house. It had no air conditioning. One night it was so hot that I dreamt that I was in an oven. I got up and took a cold shower and went back to sleep. We slept on the floor until we could find a box springs by the curb and drag that upstairs to sleep on that. It was crazy but we loved it. When we first arrived the blue light beams were shining up from Ground Zero representing the Trade Towers. I was able to bring Sean and Jordan out to see New York and they loved it. Like Sean said when they came out to visit me. "It's not that NY people aren't friendly, there's just so many people you can't say "hi" to everyone. As he imitated "Hi! Hi! Hi!" ha He was exactly right. Even though Sean wasn't real keen about coming out to see me in NY (I always went home on my days off) both he and Jordan thoroughly enjoyed their visit. They came out prior to their July birthdays and it was hot as Haiti. We went down to Ground Zero where it was still fresh from 9/11 with pictures and momentos . Jordan said it really hit him hard to be there where it had seemed more surreal before. We took the Long Island train into Penn Station, walked all over Manhattan, took yellow cabs, subways and buses all around to see the sites. We especially had fun in Central Park where an artist did caricatures of them. My kids saw it all including a homeless man sleeping on a church's front steps. I am so glad they were able to come out and they ended up saying that New York had it all. They loved Canal Street where they could buy knockout Oakley sunglasses and cheap CDs. It was fun watching them barter with the vendors.

I fell in love with flying out of JFK International because most of the time it was on dual aisle Boeing 767s with large crews going from coast to coast (called transcons) and with great layovers. We boarded up once and flew one long leg and had a great long layover and would head back to NY the next day. When we were done with our services onboard, there was always crew giving massages or a Mary Kay makeover parties etc. in the back galley. All we had to do for the last service was bake and serve cookies the last hour of the flight. My favorite transcon layover was the Westin in Long Beach, CA with a pool on the 5th floor overlooking the ocean. It had the "heavenly beds" that were fabulous. One time a stupid flight attendant took an empty rollaboard (suitcase) there and stole the comforter. Of course they caught her and fired her! Good grief. They do have a catalog where you can purchase the sheets, pillows and any of the bedding if you wish.

I got my folks to come out and visit me in N.Y. and we took an amazing tour. There were only about eight of us in an extended van and the tour guide knew the ins and outs of the city. We saw Ground Zero and took a ferry to Ellis Island where Mom put in an ancestor name on her Irish side and Dad put in an ancestor on his Dutch side and we saw their signatures to come into our country and a picture of the ship they came on... the ships looked like the Titanic. That was so interesting and then we experienced a delicious deli sandwich with a kosher dill pickle from one of the many awesome family owned delis in New York. I especially love the pizza and bagels in NY...it is the spring water that make them so good. We got to go inside the United Nations building across from the Trump Tower. Mom bought me a necklace which was supposed to bring me good luck. It looked like a turquoise ceramic beetle on a leather holder. I would later throw it around my neck while helping my Mom through Hospice and it did bring me good luck. We read in the news that a destraught filipino man opened fire outside the UN the next day so were glad we weren't part of that. Mom and I got to go up to the Observation deck of the Empire State Building but Dad didn't want to go up that high...9/11 still made him worry about heights like that. It was a picture perfect day weatherwise and we could see for miles. It was so beautiful and I took wonderful pictures of it. The tour took us down Manhattan's Fifth Avenue and Mom and I got to go into St. Patrick's Cathedral. To think that John F. Kennedy and Jackie had gotten married there and Pope John Paul had been there and took it all in. The only place we didn't touch on was Central Park. Mom and Dad enjoyed it all so much and when we got home, we couldn't believe we had been there when we saw pictures of it on the Evening News. My Dad was so fun and sweet and he had a couple of cute black gals on a bus heard us talking about him being married 50 years. They said he had the prettiest blue eyes and complimented him...it was so cute because he didn't know what to say.

American Eagle training was four weeks long. I got based at Chicago O'Hare. This was closest to home for me. I had to adjust to flying alot more to match the money I made at AA and we were on smaller aircraft. My friend Mary Kay and I bawled through the graduation because we missed AA so much. At first I was unhappy about it but I made alot of friends and we were a closer knit family with smaller crews and I became attached to it. I still had all the benefits I had at American so it was a good fit at the time. Down the road American started calling back furloughed flight attendants again but I decided to stay put...my parents were getting older and I didn't want to go on reserve again where I wouldn't have a schedule. I wanted to be able to be around to help with them as they grew older. I stayed at American Eagle and it's name would change to Envoy Air and I was glad I had stayed.

When I first started flying at American Eagle there was a pilot that was always stalking me. He appeared out of no where alot and always sat close to where I was in the breakroom and ended up getting a crashpad in the same motel where I was. He was always helpful if I needed help on the computer. He was very smart. I think he thought I was younger than I was. He was going through a divorce and he had a son. He was talented in fashion merchandising and cooking. I went out to the pool one day at the motel and the next thing I knew he was sitting next to me. I enjoyed his company but I wasn't interested...I was going with someone back home and he eventually caught on to that. I discovered he was a very promiscuous type as he had many women waiting in the corners for him if he needed them.

We were landing at Dallas Fort Worth (DFW) airport one day and there were tornado warnings out. The clouds were spooky and yellowish. There was a new hire First Officer landing and the aircraft had attitude. Airplane attitude is based on relative positions of the nose and wings on the natural horizon. At any rate it felt strange and not normal. I was the #1 flight attendant up front and the #2 was down the aisle from me. We could see each other and he was at an weird angle to me...it was strange. The First Officer even said he was nervous. I was so glad to be safely on the ground...I wondered why they would ever have us land in such conditions.

On a long layover in Memphis, TN I went to Graceland. There was a tour guide that took us through Elvis's house and to where the family was buried. The house was grossly decorated in the 70's decor with a jungle room and looked like Tarzan might swing through it at any minute. The recreation room had navy and yellow vinyl covered furniture and the livingroom had the longest couch in the world. It really struck me that he truly was the "King of Rock 'n' Roll" when I went through the buildings with all his outfits. The horses in the pastures were beautiful. The graves of Elvis & his parents were covered with flowers as it was the anniversary of Elvis's death.

My youngest son J called me at 1 a.m. while I was on a layover in Louisville, KY and said the CO detector was going off and he wondered what to do. I said get Bear and get out of the house and call the Fire Department. Sure enough there was carbon monoxide coming out of the furnace in the garage that heats the diningroom. When the inspector had come to the house before I bought it he didn't know there was a furnace in the garage. Thank God I didn't lose my son and dog. I wrote an article in the paper to tell people to please get a CO detector and make sure the batteries are good in it. We hadn't lived there very long when this happened and I got pneumonia for the first time in my life due to being exhausted from moving in the winter and not being able to take any time off. In Milwaukee we had boarded the plane when it was 30 below zero and it was not preheated. I never got warm all day and when I got home I took a hot soaker but still got sick. I had bought all new appliances when I moved in and that dipped into the money that I had made on my older home which wasn't alot. When this happened to the furnace it made it impossible to make ends meet so I went to the bank to get a loan. I was trying to increase my mortgage payment so I could pay for the new furnace and get back on my feet again. We had just lost Hayden, S was back in Iraq and Dad was dying...I couldn't think.

I had a serious crush on a single Embriar 145 Captain at American Eagle. We had chemistry. Every time he walked into the breakroom my heart would almost flip. We were sabre stalking each other which meant we were checking each other's flying schedules. Every time I would come off a plane he would walk by my gate or be hanging out by it. He was well built, had slightly balding black hair, gorgeous eyes, big mustache and carried himself well always looking very dapper in his uniform and hat. He lived on a lake by Minneapolis... what ?? That would be my dream come true! He was a real man. I would have the other flight attendants that flew with him tell me what he was like. Then I finally got to fly with him. He landed that jet so softly I could hardly feel it touch down. We would visit between flights and one time he turned around in the cockpit and just stared into my eyes...talk about want to melt. He would watch me clean the plane between flights. I think he liked me. This was the trip when my first grandchild Jack was born and I had put in to get off a day early so I could bring Jack and his Mama home from the hospital. I was walking down the corridor to leave and Captain 'Studman' came running up to me and said that I had gotten junior manned and couldn't leave. Junior manned meant that scheduling had put more flying onto my schedule. He meant he wanted me to stay on the trip. I looked at him and then I realized that he was kidding me. I found out he had a former flight attendant living with him and she worked at the Harley Davidson and he had a Harley. Why is it that men must have their cake and eat it too? They usually want the woman to pursue them and they don't give up what they've got until they have something else! I sound like Carrie Bradshaw from Sex and the City. I am old school and liked to be chased. He ended up going out to work for the Union in D.C. and I didn't see him except in Union magazines. I will always wonder what would have happened if I would have shown him I was interested.

Many fun times and new adventures happened. When the highlight of my life happened... the birth of my first grandchild Jackson James I was handing out chocolate cigars to passengers and real cigars to my crew that smoked. I was on top of the world. The only bad thing was that S was at Army boot camp when Jackson was born. I bought a Kodak instant developer so I could send S those first pictures faster. I remember driving K and Jack home from the hospital and feeling sorry for K...she cried and I know she wanted S with her. S told me he got called up to the front of his class and he thought he was in trouble and the Sergeant put his face up to S's face and started yelling " Jackson James born February 15th 2005 etc." and it was all S could do not to cry...I thought that should be in a movie. I had written S that my Dad had said that S was the first thing he thought of in the morning and the last thing he thought about at night. That choked him up too. Mom, Dad, J, and I went down to S's graduation from Camp Leonard Wood (aka Lost in the Woods). K told me she had driven in some awful weather...

thank you God for getting them down there safely...she had precious cargo with Baby Jack in there.

All the family stood outside and we could hear the soldiers coming up and down the hills before they got in front of us. It was so cool. Then we finally got to hug and see S...and he finally got to see little baby Jack!! It wasn't for long but it was better than nothing. S came home and worked and the Iraq War was going on. So in July 2009 I had a meal for S and had K's family over and we had to say goodbye. I remember Dad starting to cry and Jack trying to get into to the car to hug his Dad once more before he and K drove off. It was awful. But K as pregnant with their second child so we had something to look forward to.

By October K had a doctor appointment and was told to come back because the assistant sensed something was wrong and wanted to have the doctor look at the ultrasound. She found out that things didn't appear to be forming right. She came over to tell me and I knelt at her side and hugged her. We all prayed that things would work out. When she told S he lost 10 pounds and was a mess. Poor kid was half way around the world and trying to concentrate on what he had to do with this on his mind. We were told that he (Hayden) wouldn't probably not go past 25 weeks in the womb and he went 33-1/2 weeks. K ended up driving herself up to St. Mary's Hospital in Rochester, MN (the Mayo Clinic operates it) and she had an emergency C-section on January 10th. I had commuted to Chicago out of Rochester, MN that week so when I came home I flew into RST and went to see Hayden. K's Mom had called me and told me he was here but I never heard any details until I got there. H's middle name was Dad's middle name and he had tumors in his head and was blind, had 4 toes on each foot, had no rectum.... basically the only thing that was right with Hayden were his lungs and kidneys. Mayo managed to keep him alive with four medicines for a week while they studied him. I was so proud of the kids that they hadn't aborted him. Mayo was able to find out that the X chromosome was not on K's gene right and things did not develop correctly. They were able to go back and resolve cases and prevent this from happening in future cases. St. H is what I called him. This baby had purpose but ohhh the heartache. I had always prayed that I would die before my kids but I never dreamt I would see my kids bury a child.

S got home from Iraq to meet H and I went out to the airport to get him once but he wasn't on that plane...poor K needed him so badly...I could see her disappointment when I had to tell her he wasn't on that plane. He finally did make it and K and Jackson had been staying in the Ronald McDonald House which I will always be grateful for keeping them safe and close to H at this time. S and K had us all up and wear black to say goodbye to H on January 16th...a day before Mom's birthday We were told to wear black and 'Now I Lay Me Down To Sleep Photography' was there to take pictures all day. Mayo had made foot imprints of H as a keepsake for them to take home. We all held H and K even mentioned that my Dad who was suffering from Dementia but wanted to go meet H said how sorry he was and hugged her. She said how normal Dad seemed. When we left I asked a nurse how long after they pulled the air tube from him would it be and she said probably 20 minutes. Little H had such fight that he lived till the next day. There was such a glow of God in the room where S, K and Jackson were with him. I remember Mom saying that he had died on her birthday...but

I said that he went to Heaven on her birthday. S & K decided that they just wanted a small private service for H at the funeral home. They had pictures on a laptop that the photographers had taken and played Godspeed by Dixie Chicks...that was a killer. I arranged to have a little meal afterward in the Zastrow Room at the library. I remember my Dad and the other great Grandpa being there and my Dad looked at Hefty and said "What are we doing here?" It was less than three months later that Dad passed away and it was almost comforting to me to have Dad be in Heaven with H. I had no doubt that they were there together.

One of the best things my Dad ever told me before he got Dementia was that I was the cheapest of four children to raise. I was the youngest by many years and always thought that I was spoiled. He said that I never asked for any money because I worked since I was in seventh grade. I was the most active in school activities and got the best grades and first to ever get on the National Honor Society and get a March of Dimes scholarship. I was spoiled to get to spend more quality time with my parents than the others of which I will always be grateful for that time.

Dad had dementia and had to go to the nursing home because he was keeping Mom up all night and she couldn't take it any longer. He was only there a little over two weeks. He had thrown up and it aspirated into his lungs and he got pneumonia. When I first got home he couldn't breath and it was miserable to watch. They got that under control...even when he couldn't really talk, he managed to get it out that he loved me. My good friend and I spent one of the nights with him... he loved hanging out with us when we were doing projects for the Elks or wherever and laughed with us and told stories. We talked alot of the night and knew he could hear us so we reminiscenced old times. I learned that Hospice patients hear and feel pain till the very end.

Dad passed away and we had a nice funeral for him. Msgr Stanley who was close with my parents assisted Fr. Carl with the funeral. I wanted "I Can Only Imagine" by Mercy Me played at the funeral. The church was pretty full and the grandchildren were the pallbearers. One morning after the funeral Mom saw the curtains move in her bedroom and felt something touch her hand... She believed Dad was checking on her. Another time when she was at the cemetary before I took her on a trip out east to see family she saw a flash of Dad ...almost like he was saying to have a good trip. After everyone had gone home, I was sure we would lose Mom next so I would go down on my days off and have coffee with Mom and do everything to try to prevent her feeling a void. Mom's balance seemed to have been affected by her lack of sleep. She really needed to use a cane or walker but it was difficult to get her to use them. She fell and dislocated her shoulder and had to have it put back in the socket...she did that more that once and the orthopedic surgeon said if she did it one more time, she'd have to have surgery. She started using a cane. A cane didn't keep her from falling either and she fell at my son's house in Pella and broke the top of her femur and had to have a rod put in it. I took time off work as I always did and stayed in the hospital with her and helped her eat till she got stronger. S and K lived near Pella now and we were at the Tulip Festival. When Mom got home she continued using her walker and it was determined after awhile that she needed more help so she moved into an assisted living facility. She sold her house

and seemed to like it there ok but then it started to depress her...
her friends there were dying and the staff wouldn't even tell her
what happened to them when they would leave by ambulance. It
was getting expensive and she was going to have to go on Med-
icaid. I told her that she could move in with me...I had gotten a
home close to theirs and a ranch style in case one or the other
of them needed to move in with me. Mom didn't have to think
about it...she quickly said "YES!" Let the fun begin. My friends
took her under their wings and saw what a fun & faithful lady
she was. She had so much company and enjoyed it. No one was
getting her up at 6 a.m. and she loved my cooking. She slept so
good in her own bed and could go to bed whenever she wanted
to...it was like having a new freedom.

I started selling Zrii which is a juice that had some real healthy
benefits. I thought it was my way to success in the fact that I
believed in the products and the money it would generate in
my life. The girl who I was involved with in it was a huge Bon
Jovi lover. She had tickets to a concert in Chicago and wanted
me to go. I said I would get a hotel room for us with my airline
discount and we went. It was in the huge magnificient Chicago
Bears stadium. It was a great concert with Kid Rock opening
for Bon Jovi. When it was over we tried to get a cab back to the
hotel by the airport. Every time we told the cab drivers where
we were going they would lock their doors and drive off. I never
saw anything like it. Here we were alone by Soldier Field at
12:30 a.m. Out of the blue came a nice lady in a little sports car
and picked us up and dropped us off at the L train and we took
that back to the airport and then on to the hotel. The cab drivers didn't want to take us way up to the airport and miss out on
alot of short runs. I thought that should be illegal to do. I found

out that the lady I was selling Zrii with was lying to me about some things and I quit. I was so upset about that I was almost sick. I really did enjoy the product.

Mom wasn't feeling good one day when I was out flying. J took her to the emergency and her blood pressure was low and she was in alot of pain. J lived with me until his last semester of college so it was nice to have him around to watch the house and help Mom if needed. It was determined that she had diverticulitis and she was treated and released. She didn't get any better and she had been checked in town twice and they didn't have equipment to detect any further. I called St. Mary's Hospital in Rochester, MN and told them that I was driving her up. I drove her up to the emergency room and they found she had a hole in her colon. They had the equipment to detect it where our small hospital didn't...they saved her!!

Mom was still in the assisted living when she fell under her bathroom sink and broke the top of her other femur. I was up in Rochester waiting to fly into work in Chicago when I got the call that the ambulance was on the way up to Rochester with her. I called and got off work and was at the emergency room before she was. She had a rod put in her other leg. She was in so much pain. Her room was just below the heliport and there had been a bad accident so we heard the helicopter landing all day long and her surgery was delayed for a day so they could take care of the wounded accident victims. Mom's sister and husband drove up to see Mom. I was lucky enough to be able to sleep in Mom's room and there was a shower in the bathroom so I didn't have to put out money on a hotel room. My grandson was born back home while we were still at St. Mary's. I remember crying because they had named his middle name Dale after Dad. I came home and held Jacob in the hospital and took the mother gifts.

Mom has had two rods put in her legs and had a hole in her colon, diverticulosis and was always fighting UTIs...really that was the only thing she had against her. She didn't take any medicine except when she had a bladder infection.

On one of my flights our jet got struck by lightning right on the nose of the plane. It was a rough storm and I had to be seated. When it struck there was a huge boom and people screamed. Luckily aircraft are built to withstand lightning strikes but it is still a scary thing to happen. Other things like "bird strikes" would happen where a bird would fly into the engine. We would have to have the engine inspected to be sure if it would function properly on the next flight. I remember going down the runway to take off and suddenly coming to a rapid stop. That was always bewildering because what had caused that? It usually was that a few deer had wondered onto the runway or we have to wait for an aircraft to land at the last minute.

Bedbugs became a problem at the airlines. One of my friends had to switch rooms because his lock didn't work on his door. The room they switched him to had a nest of bedbugs under the bed. It was estimated that he had been bit over 300 times by over 100 bedbugs. That traumatized me. He showed me pictures of his legs and arms and back. He said it was torture to take a bath. I lost alot of sleep over this. I would check my bed thoroughly but sometimes would still wake up in the night and check again. I heard where Bounce dryer sheets prevented them so I carried a box of them with me and put two in the bed under me before I went to sleep. I never got bit.

My airline career was so healthy for me...I could listen to other flight attendant's problems and forget about mine or share my dispair with coworkers and that was therapeutic. It went through one ear and out the other because they didn't know any of these people I talked about. I had good flight attendant friends named Ann and Yumi. Ann was from Korea and Yumi was from Japan. They were always fun to plan things with and fun to fly with. They were caring and loving and I cherished them. When I retire I plan to go to a Korean spa with them and go to their home country with them someday. Wendy was another great friend from Canada... she embroidered alot during our breaks and is a fantastic artist. You could literally walk into her canvases.

My boys were not too good to me as far as keeping the house clean and etc. when I was gone. They had said they would support me if I did this career. I would come home and there would be dirty dishes in the sink and the hardwood floors would be covered with dog hair. Other flight attendants would tell me how their kids would have the house cleaned and even a meal prepared when they got home. I always thought "why don't mine?" I never got mad at them but I'd mop the floors with my uniform still on and let it go. I guess I felt guilty about all they had gone through with the divorce and with their Dad and all. They had said they supported me but I wonder if J resented me because he did say once that he didn't think I had tried hard enough to find a job around here. I thought I had but most good paying jobs took more schooling and I didn't feel I had the time or money to do that. Our communication was not always the best and that was not good. J was my quiet son...he never wanted for anything and that made me want to buy him things more...I truly adored him.

Everyone always wants to hear about adventures of being flight attendant. There are too many to recall all of them but will tell the major ones that stick in my mind. When I started this career, I turned 43 at training. I guess I was still desirable on some layovers my phone would ring at 12:30 am and I knew it was the Captain's voice but I acted like I didn't. He would say " Jayne are you awake?" I would say "NO" and hang up. These guys would want to hop in bed with me...ugh. I was on one trip when the four of us (two pilots and two flight attendants) got pretty drunk. The first officer told me that the other flight attendant was knocking on his door around 12:30 am and he never answered it...what was it with 12:30 am ??? I knew alot of this was going on but I didn't want to know about it. If you got a reputation for this at the airlines, you would never outlive it.

I had a guy I was seeing back home but we had broke up which we did alot. I flew with two guys and we had some fun layovers like Albany NY. Albany had Maxie's bar & had karoake and the first officer told me he'd take me there. The captain lived in Albany and would go home. So T and I walked across the parking lot from the hotel to Maxie's. We had a good sandwich and I sang "I Will Always Love You" by Whitney Houston and we had fun. The next day at our layover he asked me to come down and watch a movie...I said "Ok" and then he said "I will be naked." I thought he was kidding me. He wasn't. He had a great body and was not modest. He told me whenever he could find a nudist colony he would go there. He hated to wear clothes. Here's me....shy as hell and I would have to wear underwear at a nudist colony. HA He wanted to see my breasts and I thought oh what the hell and we fooled around alittle but we didn't have sex. I found out the next day that he was married but didn't wear a ring. We ended up on our last layover and the pilots and I went over to this Chinese restaurant that turns into a disco bar at night. It was crazy and kind of scary...we had a drink and left...we were the only white ones in the place and T told us we wouldn't believe what they are doing in the bathroom. The guys were huge and looked mean...we didn't stay there long. I did kind of envy how open T was with his sexuality...I certainly wasn't.

I got back together with the guy I dated in my hometown but that wasn't going to go anywhere either because he drank too much. I had hopes of going to the Caribbean and things like that with him but he wasn't gonna leave home. He couldn't even come over when I needed help getting some bats out of my house because he didn't want an DUI (driving under the influence). We had alot of fun and he was always buying me negligees but the fun ended there. I spent too much time with him and I guess I thought I was finding my kids a new Dad but that was never going to happen with him. When I started dating this guy and Dad called him a fartass...I should have listened. Ironically I just could never see any of his issues at first or didn't want to.

I formed a prayer bunch of my closest faithful friends. I entertained them alot with meals and we would tell about people that needed our prayers and pray for them. They ranged in age from in their fifties to their eighties. Margaret was the one who really instilled in me how important prayer was and gave me the Jesus Saying devotional book by Sarah Young (you can buy them at Hobby Lobby)...we called ourselves the Heavenly Seven. Those people though some have moved out of town will always be some of the most important support people in my life and still are. God truly blessed me with them and they took my Mom under their wings once Mom moved in with me and was a part of the group. Thank you Sally, Ann, Margaret, Georgie, Jeannine, and Angela for being there for me through so many bad times as well as the good times.

I met alot of celebrities when I was at the airlines and I always got excited about it for some reason it was really thrilling to me. I especially liked it when they would visit and were nice. I have their names in a book ...here's the list. Brooke Shields, Carson Daley, Joan Rivers, George Thorogood, Mini Me (Verne Troyer), Jeffrey Dean Morgan, Joan Lunden, former First Lady Laura Bush, Anthony Anderson, Wayne Brady, Chris Soules (Bachelor) Ben Carson, Kirk Ferentz (Iowa Football coach), Steadman Graham, Colby from Survivors, Dorm Roberts of the NY Jets, Carrie Fisher, Judd Hirsch, George Wendt, Donna Reed's son, Walter Cronkite, Kenyon Martin and Kevin Simmons from the NY Nets, Marie Osmond, Ted Kopple, Lynn Redgrave, Edgar WInter & band, Mike Tyson, Robert Kennedy Jr., Wolfgang Puck, Prime Minister Spencer and his wife of Antigua, Trace Atkins, Jenaro Parson of the Chicago Bulls, Wayne Brady, Rick Springfield Band and the Goo Goo Dolls Band. It was an absolute thrill to serve Walter Cronkite an ice cream sundae..I remembered him announcing that JFK passed away when I was in first grade. He was an icon and one of the anchorman of national news that we felt we could trust. He was very pleasant and I told him it was an honor to serve him and it was. I had Laura Bush on board just after she was our First Lady...there were five secret service men onboard. One in the cockpit, one across the aisle from her and her assistant, three in the row behind her. I asked the pilot why was there one in the cockpit and it was so the pilots didn't try to take down the plane. Oh my gosh...ok...yikes.

Meeting Mini Me (Verne Troyer) was a treat for me ...I loved Austin Power's Goldmember movie that he was in. He was in first class and his feet were still several inches from reaching the edge of the seat. His smile would win your heart. He had to have assistance when he went to the lavatory because he wasn't tall enough to latch the lock. He enjoyed some red wine and when I asked him if they were making another movie he said that was up to Mike Myers ...he had arranged for a four wheeler to pick him up at the gate because he didn't want to be in a wheelchair. He was only 2'8" tall and passed away not too long after our visit...his body started to shut down from a long history with alcohol. God bless you Verne.

George Wendt who played Norm on Cheers and I almost hit face to face in first class. He was seeing a child off and he was so sweet. I had the best talk with Lynn Redgrave. She was a beautiful woman and had just talked at a University in Illiniois about breast cancer that she had been fighting. She said her son was a pilot in NY and she was extremely interested in hearing about the Stony Point Players in my hometown and the productions we were doing. I heard she succumbed to her cancer in May of 2010... what a terrible loss.

The celebrity that I had onboard that made everyone jealous was Jeffrey Dean Morgan. He played Negan on the Walking Dead. He also starred on Grey's Anatomy and P.S. I Love You and others. We took a selfie and when he put his arms around me I almost melted. He was so sweet and told me about their living farm. Chickens were there for the eggs, cows were for milk...he flew into the White Plains, NY airport and lived in that area. Marie Osmond had been in Texas with her dolls and was flying on back to Dallas area. She was across the aisle from me when I was deadheading (which meant I was flying in uniform but not working) and I could see how beautiful she was. She didn't feel well so I didn't get to talk to her. Rick Springfield and his band were flying into Waterloo from Chicago when I was going home. One of the members of the band cut the worst raunchious fart that I have ever smelled in my life. The whole plane were holding their noses the entire 50 minute flight. I told them that we deserved free tickets to their show for what he put us through. Rick was cute as ever.

We were deicing in Rochester, MN and the deicer truck backfired and it sounded like a gunshot. We all jumped and we had the Prime Minister Spencer of Antigua and his wife onboard. Thank God it was not an assassination attempt. Wayne Brady from Let's Make a Deal was in First Class one time and had a blanket over his head and slept on that early flight...he thanked me for letting him sleep and gave me a great big smile. Those are the main celebrities that I saw...oh also saw Prince Williams walk through O'Hare airport once...there was such a mob around him I could hardly see him. It was always fun to see celebrities and if we had a fun conversation that made it even more special. But they are only human after all and I let them have their space if I sensed they did not want to be bothered.

I was always pretty tired at the end of a four day trip but I still had to commute home. This meant flying to either Rochester, MN (RST), Waterloo, IA (ALO) or Cedar Rapids, IA (CID) and driving from there home. One night it was late and it had snowed some heavy wet snow and I was at the Rochester airport. Out of nowhere appeared a young man with a shovel and he cleaned off my car and disappeared before I could even thank him or give him some money. Was he an angel or what??!! Oftentimes flights would be cancelled or I couldn't get on to get home and I would have to stay at the airport. If I got stuck in Chicago O'Hare (ORD) I would pray there would be a recliner I could grap to make a bed in. One night there were a bunch of cancellations so the crew lounge was full. I ended up propping myself up against the refrigerator and sleeping and praying no little mice came over by me. But by far the worse night was when I thought I could fly into Minneapolis, MN (MSP) and catch a shuttle to RST and drive home. By the time I got to MSP the shuttles had quit running and I had to spend the night in the airport. The clock chimed on every hour and half hour and there was a little mouse trying to get into my duffle bag. Every time I moved on a chair the lights came on.Ughhhhh!! I finally got settled in a bar area on a cushioned round booth. It was the worse night of trying to sleep in an airport ever!! I have so many disastrous commuting stories that I would have had to keep a journal to remember them all. I was always so grateful when I got home without any delays, cancellations, bad weather and etc. I have to mention one more odd thing that happened on my commute home. The day had been full of tornado watches, warnings and threatening weather. I was driving home from RST on the blacktops and I looked to my right. A little funnel cloud had developed and was coming down in the field next to me. The ditch was the only thing between us. It was following along beside me and then it went up and I thought it was gone. I looked over and it was coming down again!! This went on several times and finally was it was gone. I've never witnessed anything like that before and I hope I never do again. I've slept in many an airport over the years like LAX (Los Angeles International), DFW (Dallas Fort Worth), LGA (New York LaGuardia) but they had a crew lounge that I could get access to and usually had recliners to sleep in. If I were lucky some lounges had showers, coffee and refrigerators.

It's funny how everyone thinks pilots are all promiscuous but actually that is not true. Pilots come in all sizes, shapes and personalities. I flew with a pilot that was short and bowlegged. He was a good pilot but was into mail order women. Oftentimes there would be a woman waiting for him in the lobby for the overnight. He didn't want them to acknowledge him with any of the crew around. There was another pilot that I got stuck flying alot with cuz we were both on reserve. He was deranged in my opinion... I could just tell by his looks and actions. He became irrate over little things. He supposedly was into mail order brides too and would make his "wife" sit at the airport all day while he flew. He eventually got fired for hitting a little boy that came up to see the cockpit. There were the wonderful handsome and faithful pilots who were great husbands and fathers. I could dream about them but I would never mess with them or try to. However there were always those flight attendants that would try to break up those marriages and some would. There were also flight attendants that if a pilot rejected them they would make up lies and get the pilot in trouble and sometimes fired. That is evil. For the most part we were all there to work and get along and have fun when we could. Sometimes we would fly for a month together and it was like a major withdrawal when we were done with the month and had to change crews.

When I was first at American Airlines there were a couple of pilots that had transgended from men to women. I flew with the tall red headed one and had to serve her a coke and lunch in the cockpit. I was a very naive lady from Iowa with no experience in this area. It was thundering and lightning and I felt like I was in a horror movie. This Captain looked like Herman Munster with shoulder length red hair. She seemed very sweet but I couldn't help but think how it would feel to be her...is she accepted or scorned ? It was sad to me.

I had a trip that took me to Cuba!! We first flew to Miami and had to bring an interpreter with us. The flight was too turbulent to serve a beverage. When we got there the pilot said to give the employees all the almond M&Ms and Coke that we had. The rampers (who unload suitcases etc.) and the agents were so happy about receiving these treats because they did not make enough money to buy them. They were just getting hooked up to wifi and didn't have credit cards yet. We had to go through security to get into the airport and we had to have cash to buy any items. They sold rum, cigars and cheap jewelry. I bought a few cigars and some cheap bracelets to bring back to my kids and grandkids. It was amazing to hear about how Cubans live and their income. I felt sorry for them but yet hated to think of them becoming modernized too. Their leader at the time was

Raul Castro and was really into Pope Francis and that was encouraging. If our plane would have broken down we were not allowed to overnight in Cuba...we would have had to have another crew come get us. When the crew flew to Quantanamo we had to fly along the coast and could not cross over land... there were many regulations to flying to Cuba but I was fortunate to experience it once.

I have been in every state in the US except Vermont, Wyoming and Alaska...because we didn't fly to Wyoming or Vermont. I was in every major city in Canada except for Vancouver and I went to the Caribbean but boycotted Mexico because I was afraid of the Cartell. Many crews had scary things happen to them in Mexico and without cell phone usage they were like sitting ducks... no thanks. On our four day trips we always had at least one day that was a long day and we could get out and see the city. One time I had a "lost day" in Nashville TN. A lost day was when you would get into the layover one night and not fly anywhere the next day and leave the 3rd day early. I knew the flight attendant for the Nashville lost day and we ventured downtown and got on a tour that took us all around the town and told us history. We had so much fun and listened to great country music and ate great BBQ. We were gonna go to the Grand Ol' Opry to hear Keith Urban and Darious Rucker but we had to get up at 3 am and we didn't think we could handle it. Well I didn't sleep good and wish now I would have gone.

I was on a long layover in Canada and it was the first time that I was ever at Calgary. I had a fun crew and we decided to rent a minivan and go exploring. It took us 1-1/2 hours to get over to Lake Louise...the Rocky Mountains were breathtaking.

We spent quite awhile there and decided to climb a waterfall. I was a little nervous because they didn't give us mace to ward off Bears or wild animals but there was a fence along the trail so that helped. We went to Banff and ate supper. Banff is a town of 7,847 but all the restaurants were so crowded it took us awhile to get in any place. It's a great tourist area and popular for the majestic mountains and endless outdoor adventures. It was amazing. We got back to the hotel at midnight and had to get up at 3 a.m. The other flight attendant and I knocked on each other walls to be sure we were up. It was worth it!! Another very good friend of mine was Wendy and she was from the Toronto area.

New Orleans was another fun layover. I loved the atmosphere. We would start on Bourbon Street and go from there. There was the Cat's Meow that served 3 to 1 drinks and we could sing karoake. Every place had music..all different kinds and it was all fabulous. We found in later years that Boubon Street was getting kind of raunchy. Twice I had the same transgender scare me by popping in front of my face and saying "Can I take your picture?" Creeped me out and I didn't like it. I almost had my backpack taken cuz it was hanging from one shoulder and the flight attendant saw someone coming for it. We ended up going to the French Quarters to eat and hang out...great food, music and safer. The real estate down in that area is great too. Cafe Du Monde is a must stop to get a warm beignet. A beignet is a French deep fried pastry that is served warm with powdered sugar sprinkled on top. New Orleans is alittle Las Vegas with their casinos, alittle New York with their Saks and 5th Avenue stores and like France with their architecture and

French cruisine. I love the feather boas, beads, masks and the Saints. It's just a fun place but you have to be careful.

When S graduated from High School in 2003 he said he wanted to go to Hawaii. I had tears in my eyes when we landed in Honolulu. I couldn't believe I had actually got my kids there... thanks to my airline job. We had my airline son Andre who lived there tour guide us and the boys snorkled and we went to North Shore where they surf in January but the waves were pretty good size even in June. S had sand impacked into his groin area from being out in the waves and could hardly walk. It was funny. J had his picture taken with a huge tuna and we got leied on the beach...that is we each got a flower lei by giving a donation to the ones who made them. It was such a fabulous trip...the boys got first class both ways and I toughed it out in coach. Eight and a half hour nonstop from Chicago to Honolulu. I always said I could go back each year but never have...yet.

My kids got to see Chicago, New York City, Dallas, Honolulu and the Christmas before S left for Iraq, we went to Disneyland in California. The winter weather messed up our flights because we didn't make it to our second flight in Chicago in time and we got rolled five times we finally got on and we all got in first class!! I remember Jordan looking at me and saying "Sweet". Jackson sat like a little angel with his Curious George while another little boy ran up and down the aisle most of the trip. Jack was only three years old. I've always been so proud of him. We had to fly to Los Angeles and take a shuttle to Santa Ana. We saw the Disney parade on Christmas Day, rode all the rides, got soveneirs and had a nice hotel with a pool. I took them to the In & Out Burger but my kids didn't care for it much. It was fun to see Christmas decorations and lights out in California where they don't have snow. They really decorate ornately. It was a fun trip and a memorable one.

I moved from the house I raised my boys on 3rd Avenue to J Street in Dec 2007. S sold me the house as he was a realtor at the time. One of my new neighbors became one of my dearest friends to date. She loved animals as much as I did and had three dogs...two that were rescues and one that was her son's. Her oldest son was shot to death by his neighbor who had PTSD from being in Iraq. It is an unimaginable grief to hold a friend who has lost a child in such a senseless way.

Not often did I have passengers from my hometown onboard because most took Delta out of Minneapolis which was closer to home. But on one trip I was doing a beverage service and when I got to the back I recognized a lady from home. "Louise?" I said. It was Louise and she was going to some place out east to see an infant grandson who had heart problems. I gave her some snacks and offered her to stay over with the crew if she was too tired to drive further. She told me the story and rested and felt up to traveling on...we saw each other at a St. Patrick's Day celebration and she grabbed me and hugged me so tight and thanked me for that night. Her grandson is doing well. It was good to find that out because so often we hear passenger's stories and never find out the outcome. I had a pastor and his wife that were my neighbors on 3rd Avenue onboard, a doctor and his wife and a farmer's wife from my area and an ex-superintendant from my town onboard as well. Pastor Downey said a prayer with me before takeoff for my Mom who was not feeling too good at the time. It comforted me.

Other popular layovers were San Diego Caifornia. Our crew went to see the USS Midway at Seaport. The Captain bent each of us over like he was kissing us by the statue with the sailor and nurse kissing and celebrating the end of WWII in New York Time's Square in 1945. He had snuff in his mouth but he did not drip it on us. He was alittle looped and was squirting lobster all over the place. I'm not a lobster person...prefer shrimp. It was a great layover and weather. We flew our butts off the next day to make up for that lost day. I also enjoyed going to Los Angeles. There were always tours you could take of Beverly Hills, etc. My friend was on a layover that went to the wax museum and it was the day that they unveiled Betty White' statue and she was there!!! Oh what a memory that would have been. The hotel was nice where we stayed in LA but this homeless guy was always hanging around. I'd go to the Subway and his long body would be stretched across the sidewalk. I was prepared to get him a sandwich if he woke...never want to give them money that they could spend on drugs or alcohol but I lucked out and he didn't wake up. There was a bus you could take from the hotel to Santa Barbara and go shopping or go to Manhattan beach. Loved the weather and to get away especially in the winter. I loved flying back and seeing the topography of our country from the beach to the mountains to the plains etc. I usually had a little jet lag coming back from the west coast too...extra tired for a day.

We added Montana as a state to fly into. What fun we would have. The mountains were beautiful and I loved visiting with the passengers that would go there for vacation. People would say they rented a cabin and would horseback ride and hike and never turn on the television or radio and loved it...a total escape. Another western layover was Denver, CO. I never was wild about this airport...it was supposed to look like a snow capped mountain but I thought it looked more like a circus carnival tent. The red eyes of the horse statue outside freaked me out and it was thought to be cursed. Some people had died putting it up. This airport was said to be built on sacred Indian burial grounds. It was built so far out of town that they used to have to shuttle us for about an hour to our hotels. They finally built some hotels closer and that was better. It's usually real bumpy taking off and landing there because of the mountains. It was never my favorite layover. I also had to practice my patience on the passengers that were high on pot. I could always tell who they were and they always seemed paranoid and they never listened to the announcements. UGHHHH

El Paso, TX was delightful. It was a nice airport and hotel with a pool. This was always nice to getaway to and it was warmer in the winter. It never failed to amaze me that no matter where we went to eat, I could never eat the salsa that they served with the chips. Even the mildest salsa made my mouth burn. I guess I am a wuss that way but we were not raised with hot jalapeno salsa in Iowa. I loved having the shuttle take us to the mall and do alittle shopping. Every morning they had a free breakfast which I loved...just had to watch out for the jalapeno salsa!! We had to be careful in El Paso because it' so close to Mexico. I also always enjoyed Phoenix AZ and Albuquerque NM layovers too. The dry climate is fun to experience but I have burned my feet on the cement by the pool in the summer out there. On a layover in Phoenix a flight attendant got free tickets and asked me to see the Chicago Cubs play the Arizona Diamondbacks play. We had great seats and got free t-shirts and had a blast. That was the year that the Diamondbacks won the World Series. This was the trip where the flight attendant I worked with in coach was a B-I-T-C-H. She knew I was a newbie and she wanted to intimidate me and she did. She looked like a big Nazi or something ..ha.. she would yell at me and say "how many meals do you have left on your cart?" I'd count and say "such and such". She'd almost scream "Are you sure?" I would almost freeze up because she was so obnoxious...it might as well been my sister onboard. Then when this gal found out I had gone to the ballgame with the number #1 flight attendant she looked at me and said "She took you ????" Oh was I glad to get off that trip.

I really enjoyed flying to San Francisco CA. It was absolutely beautiful but it was cold in July...the fog that came off the ocean made it chilly. I loved going to the Seas Candy Store (that where it originated) and shopping and eating there. One regret I have is not going to "Paint Your Wagon" play when Robert Goulet starred in it out there. Alot of homeless were on benches outside the hotel when we left in the early morning. I found out that it is warmer there in September. Next time I go I would like to see Alcatraz Island.

When it comes to the richest county in the country that is White Plains, NY. I loved those layovers...fabulous older homes but beautiful and we could take a train to Manhattan which was 40 minutes away. We stayed at a Hilton and it was very nice and very expensive. I would talk to the bartenders and they told me what they paid in taxes and it is was out of sight. A man had been murdered in the hotel. Ben Novack JR was found bludgeoned, bound and gaged inside a hotel suite Room 453 at the Hilton. The fifty-three year old man of wealth was killed by his wife who was wanting to seize control of his fortune. I never sensed anything funky ghostwise in this hotel. I would love to go on a tour of homes in this area someday.

Talking about murders let me tell you about Chattanooga TN Reed Hotel. The first time I went there it hadn't been renovated yet and it was what I call "crusty". I had to leave a light on in the two room suite because I felt it was creepy. It was an old hotel that had been a hospital in the Civil War days. The main lobby had pictures of General Custer and others and it felt like their eyes moved when you did...you know...ouuuuu. Whenever I knew I was going there I packed my holy water and sprinkled it around in my room. I never had any problems until the night we slept on the third floor. I had heard all about this place and it was supposedly haunted. The story had it that prostitute Annilisa Netherly during the Civil War had her head cut off in the bath tub by a jealous lover in Room 311. It is said that if you stay in that room that she will turn the light on and off and lay on men, etc. Alot of stupid men liked to rent it just to see what happens. Al Capone used to stay in that room and would kick anyone in it out when he came to town. It had iron bars on the windows until it was renovated in 2004. Well anyway I was telling the first officer that I was flying with all about it and we were staying on that floor just doors down from Rm 311. By the way this first officer was the nicest young man from Dallas area and he was 6'9" tall. When he did the walk around to check out the aircraft, you could see his head above the wings..ha. He was a handsome "Lurch". I fell asleep that night with my clothes on which I never did. I heard a blood curdling scream at midnight and it woke me up. I chuckled to myself that some kids must have rented out that room and got scared and I went back to sleep. In the morning when I went downstairs to check out I was telling the clerk that I heard screams so were some kids in Rm 311? His eyes got big and he said "No one was in that room last night." He gave me a bunch of Sticky Finger (a BBQ restaurant there) coupons and I concluded that I must have heard the ghost. I will never forget that scream...blood curdling from the rafters...I tried to imitate it but it scared the Captain. HA I am open to the fact that there are ghosts but I don't like to get entangled in them or try to communicate with them but I definitely experienced something that night that I'll never forget. My sense of a paranormal was spot on.

I got tired of going through Canadian customs but really did enjoy Ottawa. It sits on the Ottawa River and is home to the Parliament. In the winter businessmen could be seen ice skating to work with their briefcases on the canal and in the summer there were boats in the canal. It's very picturesque. In the summer they had great farmer markets and I had to watch it that I didn't buy something that would be hard to get home on the plane. The Novotel hotel was new and clean with great amenities. We got into our overnight one time and there had been an attempt to assassinate the Prime Minister. How scary is that?! I loved Montreal, Toronto and Calgary Canada layovers but Ottawa will always be my favorite because of it's uniqueness.

I had layovers in Las Vegas but was not raised a gambler so if I couldn't see a show or go to a comedy club I was not that excited about it. Once I'd seen the different casino designs then I was done with it. It was not worth it to me to go there just to lay out by the pool.

I have experienced all sorts of flight attendants...some were great and some were not. Some I actually wondered how they ever got hired. I flew with a gal one time from New York. I was told by people who had flown with her in NY that she once greeted passengers by holding a stuffed cat and asked "Do you want to pet my pussy?" Now I would have been fired for that. She told me she hadn't had sex in 26 years (she was 46) and I thought " I can see why". She also would put silver glitter on her chest hence she got nicknamed "Glitter". She was pretty nice to fly with but one time she got all freaked out. She was working first class and had me come up because she was concerned about a passenger. She told me that a woman had ordered to have breakfast twice. I said "What?" She said that the gal in 3C had wanted another breakfast even though she's already had one. Well I investigated and the lady had not had her breakfast yet...I don't know where Glitter's mind was but that was weird.

I flew with some flight attendants that were so wonderful and fun and we would laugh all the time and we got so many good letters and above and beyond slips from our Advantage members. Those trips would go by so fast and usually without any stress and passengers could sense our good rapport. It sets a great atmosphere on the plane with the passengers. One thing with my job my office was in the sky and if we didn't like our coworker it changed after that trip and you could avoid flying with that person again by trip trading. That doesn't happen with many jobs.

One of my favorite flight attendants was from Raleigh, NC. He was a semtress and loved dogs. He was so smart that he qualified to go on Jeopardy. He was theatrical and we just hit it off big time. We laughed most of the time. I have a video of him imitating and singing a munchkin song from Wizard of Oz. I about wet my pants. We both like to be professional and give an "above and beyond" service to our passengers. We enjoyed going out to eat with each other on our layovers and could talk for hours and hours. Jesse could describe and initate his dog and I would laugh so hard I would have tears running down my cheeks. I was working with Jesse when my dog died. I knew Bear wasn't feeling good. She had lost weight and wasn't herself. She was 10 years old and I think she had bladder cancer. I left for a trip and I had trip traded and wish I hadn't because I couldn't be there for her. My Mom and a friend took Bear to the Vet and I tried to get off my trip early but I couldn't. When we got to Atlanta I called the Vet and he told me Bear had passed away. Jesse and the Captain were huge dog lovers. They cried too. I burst into tears and when it was time to do the demo I told my passengers that I was sorry but I just found out that my dog had died. I cried just like a fountain of water was coming out of my eyes...they were all so sympathetic. When I got home I searched for some of Bear's hair to keep and I hated that she died alone. It took me a long time to get over her...perhaps you never really do.

When I was still in the crashpad phase, I had to work Christmas and New Years. I think it is funny how you never forget the time you watch the ball come down in Time Square while in pajamas with people that have become your airline family. Patrick will always have a special place in my heart. He lived in El Paso before moving to Chicago. He was a great baker and good with plants. His calm and funny rapport attracted me to him as the best bud anyone could ever have. He had the coolest Christmas vests too! One of our crashpad roommates was a United international flight attendant who commuted from Singapore to Chicago and then flew trips to China. She would have to come in a day ahead to recuperate from her commute before she would start her trip. I honestly don't know how a person can do that to their body. I couldn't.

I was always pretty mellow and always nice to my passengers but there are times when you have to be authorative. I was the first class flight attendant on a flight that we were boarding at JFK International in New York City. Catering had left me with ice that had melted and frozen in a big chunk and I had to call them to bring me new ice and everything was wild and we were trying to be on time. A big middle eastern man wanted to sit with his family and they were all spread apart. I heard a bunch of commotion and the other flight attendant wasn't agressive enough to handle it. When I went back to check it out the big guy was sitting in the Exit Row with his kids who were not 15 years old or older. It's a regulation to be at least 15 years old to sit in the Exit Row & able to operate the Exit. I had enough! I told him to "get back in your seat and get the kids in theirs and stay there and I didn't want to hear one more thing out of you." He did it and never said a word and didn't even get a beverage in flight. The other passengers almost applauded me. Thank you God!!

Minneapolis was fun to layover at. It was only a couple hours from home so friends come drive up and we could shop and spend the night. When we were at my favorite hotel we could walk to the Mall of America and Ikea. I was obsessed with Ikea. Loved their displays and most of their products and you could even eat there. I got great ideas there and loved their decor. I could spend hours in an Ikea. Ikea originated in Almhult, Sweden and their stores are worldwide. If you get a chance to go to one, do it. I especially love the three story one in Chicago. I understand some of their furniture has alot of pieces to put them together but to me it's such a treat and I'd just hire someone to do it.

Green Bay was a fun layover...sometimes our approach coming in to land I felt I could almost touch the Lambeau Field where the Packers play. Boy you didn't want to be onboard when they lost a game...they take it very seriously. The Captain bought us cheese curds one time.. did you know that if you warm them they can squeak ?! I just know that I would never want to go to a game in the dead of winter...they have no roof on their stadium....brrr

One thing I can confirm after twenty years of flying and staying in hotels and eating all sorts of food is I never got skunked on a club sandwich. They always came through for me and hit the spot when nothing else did. So remember when traveling & staying in hotels and not sure what to order to get the club, it came through for me every time!!

Flight attendants have been responsible for saving some people from human traffickers. Flight attendants have oftentimes seen irregular behavior between people and their captors on flight. Observing and carefully communicating have saved some from whatever hell they may have been subject to. Thank you God and I hope we can continue to save children and adults from this in the future.

We laid over in Atlanta, GA and the hotel was so crusty I couldn't get under the sheets or cover myself with the sheets. I layed on some towels. I looked outside in the morning and we were on a graveyard...the stones came right up to the hotel. I was so glad we moved out of there. The Westin was a huge improvement. Our overnight hotel in Oklahoma City was at an Embassy Suites. It was marvelous. If you could get there before dark you could get in on a free happy hour and if you could leave after the breakfast there was a great free buffet. The two room suites were so new and clean. I had the shuttle driver take me to the place where the bombing of the courthouse had taken place and spent part of the day there. I heard the recording of the explosion and saw all the chairs that represented each person and child that perished. It is a very solemn place and the way it was built was unique. All the chairs of the deceased were on the ground where the courthouse was. The creek that runs in front of the chairs is where the road was where the truck sat that had the explosives. The creek looked deep but was only a few inches deep...the special effects were really good. If I were to go again I would go at dusk because the chairs illuminate.

Marquette MI.. oh my gosh. When I first started flying there we stayed at an old Officer's quarters. In the winter on a long lost weekend up there (we would fly in on Friday and out on Sunday) they used to leave us the janitor's van to go skiing or golfing or into town for food. We were out in the boonies and it took 45 minutes to get there and it was a wooded area with a saw mill nearby. Of course someone abused the privileges of the van and it got taken away. This place was creepy...it had a kitchen, bathroom, livingroom and two bedrooms. I always had to leave some lights on there at night. One of my bedroom closets had a little back area that led somewhere. I never looked to see where. A flight attendant woke up and found a note on her dresser that said "You are beautiful when you sleep." That scared everyone and they moved us out of there. One time we had to park our aircraft in the hangar because it needed some repairs. When they towed us in there I looked and all these rampers looked like gnomes crawling all over the place. You could hardly tell a man from a woman and they worked super hard...it was a maintenance base. They also had a B29 sitting by the entrance of the airport and that is what my Dad flew on at the end of WWII...he was a gunner in a blister window.

One trip we were headed to Buffalo, NY. We had a cool captain that said we were going to have a great view of Niagara Falls out of the right side of the plane. We kept looking and looking and I thought we had missed it when all of a sudden it was right there!! And I mean right there!! The captain had asked for clearance to fly right by it and we did. I never desired to go see it again because this was the most awesome view of Niagara Falls you could get it was like it was so close it could suck us in....it was right there in front of us and I didn't have my camera on. The whole plane let out a huge "OHHHH"...thank you captain for getting that clearance. We will never forget it.

Many times on trips I would be taken back by passengers that had lost limps or had things they had to live with that were disabling. One incident was a veteran who entered the plane without legs...his strong arms brought him in. Then he said to me "I like your boots". An enormous amount of guilt came over me that he couldn't even wear boots. He was so courteous and didn't want any attention or sympathy. He was amazing.

Another passenger that I thought about alot was a woman from Africa that had been burned so bad it burned her hands off to her wrists. I offered to hold her soda so she could drink it but she was able to do it. I thank God everyday I didn't go through what some of these people had gone through...I can't even fathom it.

When I was still flying on reserve at Eagle, they sent me out to Los Angeles to fly. I was alone on smaller aircraft that went up and down the coast of California. I had alot of pain in my right arm and my thumb and forefinger were numb. I put ice on my arm at each layover. I went to the Mayo Clinic when I got home and found out my blood pressure was up to 200/120. I could have had a stroke. My dog had actually yanked so hard when she saw squirrels when I walked her that she had broke one of my cervical disk in my neck in three pieces. I had it removed in February of 2003 and was off work for two months.

I would have to say that the layover at the Sherry Frontenac on Miami Beach was my favorite. It's an older hotel that a family bought so that airline employees could go there and enjoy. No one under 15 years old were allowed. It was all inclusive with a bar, restaurant, breakfast theater room, fitness room, beauty parlor, massage parlor and patio with pool right on the beach. The Jackie Gleason Show was filmed just down the street. I loved it there because I loved the pool and beach option. You could walk down the block and there were great Cuban restaurants and a Publix supermarket. You could buy some meat and grill it out by the pool. There was even a beer machine that sold beer for $1.00 by the pool. One time on a trip I had forgotten to pack underwear. I had put my clean underwear back in my dresser drawer instead of my rollaboard. When I got to our layover I ran across to the Dollar General and I bought some underwear. Of course all they had were these ugly ones with a snakeskin design on them and I especially hate anything looking like snakeskin. I bought them because I wasn't going to go without underwear! Ha When I got home I threw them away.

I was having some stress at home and when I started my trip, I was working first class and a male passenger came up to me and hugged me tightly. I didn't feel threatened but instead embraced the hug. I felt like a ragdoll. He said he knew I had been under an enormous amount of stress and had been sent to tell me that " God loves you very much and not to fear". Then the man went back to his seat and I finished the rest of my service with tears in my eyes. I can't explain it any way but that it was true and very much needed.

Mom turned 90 years young on January 17, 2019 but the weather is so cold and crappy that we decided to have her party in June so more people could come. Everyone was invited and I rented the Lodge in Clear Lake, IA for the party. I had some friends cater it and we had pulled pork sandwishes, pasta salad, fruit, chips and mini cupcakes. I had a big birthday cake made for Mom too and there was a snack mix for people to munch on too. Our local nun still could not believe how many people showed up for her party and they kept coming!! Even her 90 year classmates came. It was a great time. I had rented a lake house for us to stay in for a week and my oldest nephew & family came. Achan flew in from Germany where he was working for British Petroleum for awhile. My cousin from Tennessee came and they stayed at the lake house.

When it came to performing medical and evacuation procedures on a plane it pays off to know them. It is amazing how what you learn in training comes back to you when you need it. We employees would go to Dallas every year and get recertified in AED and CPR and the evacuation drills. I never had to use the AED or do CPR but I did have some medical situations. My first one was on a flight from Chicago to El Paso, TX. There was an older couple who were heading back home from being in Poland. The gentleman had dementia and could not help us with any background information. The woman started showing signs of having a heart attack. She was sweating and had bad chest pain. I called the pilots and then announced on the PA whether there was a physician on board. There was a pediatrician that came forward to help...I checked his creditials and he had me move the lady to the floor of the bulkhead and raise her feet. She had her nitroglycerin packed in cargo...not a good thing to do. He opened the medical kit with the nitro in it and put one under her tongue. I placed a cool washcloth on her head and we keep her comfortable under we landed. The Captain had me sit in my jumpseat and the doctor to remain with the lady on the floor. We landed and the paramedics were there to get her off right away and as far as I know she survived. I wrote up all the paper work and felt good about the experience.

The next time I had a medical experience was on a big Boeing 767 coming from the West coast to New York City. A passenger in first class had a heart attack and we had to get him down fast. We landed in Colorado Springs, CO. The pilots were skilled and took that big plane down as quickly as they could without causing our noses to bleed or us to pass out. I will never forget the sound that big jet made as it came down...I was seated in the back and worked coach that trip. I was not directly involved with the ill passenger but still have to fill out some paper work being that I was part of the crew. We got him unloaded and took off and continued on our way to New York.

One time on a smaller aircraft where I was the only flight attendant I had a strange thing happen. I was serving beverages and was towards the back of the plane. All of a sudden this lady passed out and her head fell against my cart and her eyes were sort of open. She looked like a mannequin. It freaked me out...I thought she was dead. Of course when I'm stressed I always say "Oh God" or "shit". Well Oh God was coming out of my mouth and then she suddenly came to. I wanted to call paramedics to meet the plane and check her over or something but her boyfriend who was sitting across the aisle from her said "Oh she's ok...she does that sometimes!" All I could think was I hope she doesn't drive! They still had another leg to fly and I hope all went well.

On a funnier note...sometimes we would have trouble with the overhead bins on the smaller jets...they would get stuck up or down. On this jet you had to push them up to close them. There was a cute younger buff guy in the back that was struggling with the bin. So I went back there and I was saying " I CAN'T BELIEVE YOU CAN'T GET IT UP!" HA It's funniest when you don't realize what you're saying that could be interpreted another way. I said it again as I pulled the door up to shut it and turned to look at him and he said " I can't believe you just said that to me!" Then it dawned on me what I had said to him and we both laughed so hard...thank God!! I had an elderly man onboard and he wanted a Sprite during the beverage service.

The opened can of Sprite went straight up in the air and flipped upside down and landed in his lap. He just sat there and smiled the biggest smile... it must of felt good.

The Concord which was a supersonic jet that retired in 2003. It was ahead of us to take off at JFK International airport one day in 2001. As it revved up its engines to take off the ground rumbled like an earthquake... it was something to experience that. It flew from 1969 until 2003 and would cruise at 1341 mph. Our jets would cruise at between 500-575 mph so it was signficiantly faster than any other commercial jets.

Another thing that happened to me that made me realize how much I took flying for granted was when a first time flyer was onboard. He was in his thirties and I told him he might want to chew gum to keep his ears from plugging up. When we took off, he almost came up out of his seat. He was overwhelmed by the clouds and was like a little kid who got his favorite toy for Christmas. He was almost yelling and was so incredibly amazed by everything. "Oh my gosh are those the clouds?!" "Oh we are so slanted!" "I can't believe this..it is so cool!" "Wow!" It really was cute and made me think it was a really remarkable thing to fly.

I had to deal with alot of bloody noses and such but those weren't too serious. One male passenger had the worse case of anxiety that I've ever seen. It was very turbulent and that man was hanging onto the overhead bin rail above him and the back of the seat in front of him. He was miserable and just had to tough it out. It is frustrating when you really can't do much for people like that but talk calmly to them and hope that relaxes them and tell them to deep breathe. When there is turbulence I have to remain in my seat as well.

Right when I was feeling old at 59 years I got asked to dinner on a layover with a pilot who was 47 years old and he tells me that I'm hot. I didn't let him kiss me goodnight or it may have gone farther but it was fun and flattering and just what this old gal needed at the time.

I had some evacuation drills for real. One was on a flight out of Chicago O'Hare. The Captain thought that there was something wrong with the plane so we did a fly by the ATC (air traffic control tower) and then landed and took a sharp right off the runway and went bumping across grass and stopped just short of hitting some landing lights. Once we were completely stopped someone said that they could smell something hot and I accessed the front door and there was no fire so I opened it and the passengers had to jump 5'3" to the ground and move away from the aircraft. I got half of them out shouting out the commands that training had drilled into head. Then a fireman outside told me there was no fire so I could stop evacuating. Those remaining passengers were so glad that they didn't have to jump. I was so relieved that no one had gotten hurt and when it was over I had a little meltdown that everyone was safe. It's amazing how your adrenaline flows at times like that.

Another stressful flight was one into Aspen CO. The weather was very windy. We were "ferrying" the flight (which means we had no passengers onboard but had to get the plane there for the next outgoing flight). I remember asking the other flight attendant if it was always this bumpy and he said "NO". We literally felt like a salt shaker..it was bad. The pilots tried and tried to attempt to land. We finally had to land in Grand Junction CO. Come to find out that Air Traffic Control had forgot to tell us that it was too windy to land in Aspen. Ugh. I got some extra time off around Easter because of it.

If I sat in the back jumpseat of the plane, people were always going by it to get to the lavatory (what we called the restroom). One time we were going to Atlanta and a passenger didn't make it to the lav and threw up in my jumpseat. She threw up and threw up and threw up. Of course my jumpseat wasn't fit to sit in so there was an extra seat that I was able to sit on to fly back. I wonder how they ever get a jumpseat cleaned with all the straps and crevices...ugh I was glad I didn't have to clean it up.

When we layed over in Washington, D.C. we stayed up the road from the Pentagon. We could still see where American Airlines flight 77 hit the building on 9/11. Some of the employees there remembered seeing the large jet flying so low past the hotel. There was a pool on the top of that hotel...I loved that.

One of my worst experiences at the airlines was my "hard landing". We were coming in from a four day trip and I remember the new hired first officer was saying how he had a hard time getting the feel for landing since he had been a helicopter pilot. They had started hiring helicopter pilots because they were so short on pilots. He was the sweetest guy and had been active in the military overseas doing some scary flying. We came into O'Hare and the CRJ we were riding on came down and went back up again and slammed down hard on the tarmac. I was in the back jumpseat and took the brunt of it. The passengers were

screaming and crying. I even said " That was hard!" The first
officer had landed it but the captain drove it to the gate. The
other flight attendant and I got off as soon as possible and let
the paramedics handle any injured passengers. We had to put a
report in at the office and we went home. My back ended up
hurting for quite some time. I got some time off and bid to do
the number one position from then on so I would be able to
sit in the front jumpseat. We did have one more hard landing
before I retired and I was in the front jumpseat but it upset me
so much I went to the hotel room and threw up a few times.
It can really upset your system when that happens. It was said
that that particular CRJ was in maintenance for months and
never really recovered and cost milllions. Number 521...never
will forget that tail number.

Mom was starting to fail more and needed more help when the
Pandemic started. The last time I flew was March 3rd 2020...I
met a friend and her husband for drinks at Harry Carays bar at
the hotel I was staying at and then when I got home Mom had
stood up and had a bone break in her foot. I was thankful that
the airlines offered a leave every month. I took the leaves and
had to pay my healthcare in but it didn't count against my atten-
dance. When it came time for me to return to work in March
2021 Mom was having alot of UTIs (urinary tract infections)
and the ER doctor prescribed her too strong of antibiotics and
she got c-diff which was short for Clostridioides difficle which
was a germ that causes diarrhea and colitis. It was the most
disgusting thing I had ever witnessed. The stench was almost
intolerable and it was very toxic. The antibiotics had taken away
too many of her good gut bacteria and let this awful bacteria
into her system. I was on an early buy out retirement from the

airlines that would end April 1st of 2022 and I was glad. Mom was so sick it was awful. The local hospital had done as much as they could do for her and she had to go to Mayo Clinic in Rochester, MN to have them try to help her. They told us that she would have to have a fecal transplant...this involved taking stool from a healthy donor and putting it in a person infected with c-diff. I found out later that it usually takes more than one implant. I stayed in a hotel (couldn't stay in her room) and was there everyday. I came home one day to check mail and sleep in my own bed and save alittle money. But I mostly was there with her through it all. She finally got to come back home but had to be in a swing bed for several more weeks until she could get strong enough to get released. Well guess what? She got c-diff again. This time I did not think she was going to make it. She even at one point told me she didn't think she was going to make it either. She couldn't open her eyes or talk she was so sick. Her doctor chose to treat her and get instructions from Mayo and she survived...she was small but mighty.

I started a cooking show on YouTube with my friend called " Now We're Cookin'!" during the pandemic. My friend's mother fell and broke her hip and couldn't be on the show indefinitely so I continued on my own calling it "Grma Jayne's World" on YouTube.com. I hired a lady to teach me how to upload my own episodes and am continuing to film them. I am very amateur at this but have shared my family's wonderful recipes with humor and faith. I think one of the funniest episode is the Beer Can Chicken when I couldn't get the chicken on the stand. I can't believe I didn't cuss. My videos are very real! haha I have over 140 videos and over 200 subscribers so far. It was a perfect way to pass time & keep my sanity during the pandemic.

Mom finally got home and then I sold my house in July 2021. My house needed alot of things done to it and I was having a hard time getting anyone over to do the repairs and I didn't feel I needed a house anymore. It sold and I found a place to rent. Mom fell the week before we were supposed to move... she was reaching into her closet and got too far away from her walker. I heard a thump and went into her bedroom and she laid on the floor and her wrist was already swelled up. A dear friend of mine who lived in town had a couple girls that helped at nursing homes and I called them and they helped me get Mom to the hospital. She wasn't able to use her walker with a broken wrist. Mom had to go into the nursing home to recuperate. I hated it and she hated it but that was the only thing we could do. I visited her almost everyday. I went after I subbed at school. She cried and wanted out...she hated the food. I took food out to her alot. The place I was renting had been a doctor's office and the people left it filthy...most of the appliances were on their last legs. The nice LG washer and dryer were good but the dryer wasn't hooked up so I got sick from that. I looked around for a new place and couldn't wait to get out of there. I brought Mom over to see it before I moved and I could hardly get her back in the car to take her back. Her bladder infection was back!! Why wouldn't it be?? They were putting her in bed at 6:30 pm at night and letting her lay in bed till sometimes 9:30 am...of course she was wet and got bladder infection. I found out that she was talking out of her head and telling the aides to cut up her clothes and crazy stuff. I was so fricking livid!! Mom cried and told me she needed to get out of there. As soon as her wrist was healed I got her out of there. I had moved to a super nice apartment and I got her in there by Thanksgiving. Mom was good for about a month. She had to go to ER one day to have her UTI checked and it was full of people with Covid and I couldn't go in with her....she was there for five hours and I had to have the police help me get her back upstairs to my apartment. She could not talk or walk and I thought she was going to die. I sobbed all night and let her lay on her bed all night with her coat on. She had come around in the morning and was doing better. We had weird weather and had a tornado warning in December and I tried to get her down to the fallout shelter but Mom had lost the use of her legs and I could only get her down to the ground level of our fourplex. I was sure we were gonna get blown away but we survived. I called the fire department to help me get her back upstairs. Those two things really took a toll on Mom. I have to thank the police and fire departments for helping me on numerous occasions when Mom would fall. I was trying to keep her from getting Covid or c-diff in her last days and succeeded. A friend of mine who works with Hospice came out and placed Mom in Hospice care with me. That was Sunday December 12th. A few days later Hospice had a nice hospice bed set up in her room. It was a smart bed that regulated the air in the cushions and basically massaged her constantly. I could position her many ways even like she was sitting in a chair...amazing. Hospice told me that I could never leave her alone. I relied on my friends to come over and sit while I ran to the store quick. I was instructed on the administered sedatives and morphone. I wrote everything down on paper and kept everything on my wooden cutting board in the kitchen. I was very focused...probably more than I ever had been in my life. One night I got up to use the bathroom at 3:15 am and Mom was sitting in the wing chair next to her bed. She didn't have legs!! What was going on?! I said "Mom what are you doing? You have to get back in bed." She said "I do?" I said

"Yes you could fall and break something." I got her back in bed and I was very paranoid that I would see her walking into my bedroom sometime in the middle of the night but the sedative got her to relax more and she didn't try that again...praise God. When it came to giving her morphine I cried and felt like I was killing her. I text a nurse friend that I felt like Dr. Kevorkian. She said she felt like that going through Hospice with her mother years ago. She had asked Msgr. Stanley if it hastened her mother's life and he said "about 5 seconds". That was exactly what I needed to hear...Msgr Hayek was very close to my folks so that was perfect. I could do this.

While Mom was still in the nursing home I slipped out to New York to see a friend and go to the Tina Turner Musical. It was a bucket list trip that was the best ever. I took an Uber from my hotel by the airport to the first five star restaurant Baccaret to meet Tim. It was so awesome to have a guy open the door and say " Welcome to Baccaret's Ms Stowe". Oh yeah I could get used to that. The Uber driver had played Christmas music as we crossed the lighted bridges into Manhattan. It was magical. Tessie's youngest brother Tim took me out on the town the night before the musical and shopping down on 5th Avenue. I filmed the trip and aired it on my cooking show "Grma Jayne's World" on YouTube.com. It was a fabulous trip before Thanksgiving and a well needed one because I had no idea what I would go through once I got home.

I had started to sub at the schools last fall and loved it. I commited to six weeks of subbing with Level 2 children at Lincoln Stinkin'...what goes around, comes around. I loved my autistic boy A and behavior deficient girl Em. They grew on me but it was all new world to me. The teachers and staff were all great to work with. One day A caught me off guard and got away from me and ran up the stairs to some offices. I ran after him and he threw himself on his back and slid around on the floor on his back and looked like he would hit his head on the walls of the hallway. His strength had at least doubled and I couldn't get him pulled up or stopped. I kept yelling for him to STOP. He didn't and he had this horrifying deep laugh ...HA... HA... HA...talk about freaky. A AEA instructor heard this and right as I thought he was heading to a stairway going downstairs head first she came to my rescue. We got him to stand up and back to class. I discovered that at seven years of age that A was a genius. He may not always relate to what you wanted him to do etc. but he could do amazing things on the computer when you let him have at it. Like the Rain Man movie!! WOW! It was just short of the worse nightmare I had ever had. I think A liked me ...he came close to biting me a few times...even felt his teeth on my forearm once but he never did. I rubbed his back almost constantly to keep him calm but if I said "shhh" to him too much he would turn to me and say "SHHHHHH!!!" really loud. Kind of made me laugh. The little girl Em was the most defiant thing I had ever experienced in my life. It turned out her home life sucked. She had an older sister that left home and they didn't know for sure where she was. If Em didn't want to do an assignment ....come hell or high water she would not do it. We had to call to have her removed from the classroom alot. It was seldom a day would go by without that happening. I wanted to squeeze her and make things all right. She could be so darling with her happy gestures and smile. God bless these children.. they try so hard to fit in. I pray that people don't bully them and if they do that they are not affected by it. By the Grace of God go I is what I think... I could have been born this way. I have subbed on all levels now and can say that our "next generation" is in trouble. So many of them are from broken homes where there is abuse, neglect and lack of food. Nothing killed me more than feeding elementary kids on Monday mornings because a boyfriend had eaten the food sent home by the school. We had to make sure they ate before they drank too much milk because they would fill up on milk and not eat as much. What is going on ? I never thought I would see this.

I dressed up in my nun habit on my day off and thought I'd go to school and bless my 3rd graders for Halloween and give them treats. I blessed them and played kick ball with them and talked to them and wore sunglasses and they never guessed it was me!! The little naughty girl in the class grabbed my hand and said "Oh sister pray with me!" That cracked me up. I have some great pictures from that day.

I learned at a young age that if I didn't have much money, I could still make gifts for my friends and family by painting them something or making them jewelry or baking them something or simply being there for them. My favorite quote is from Mother Teresa..."Do small things with great love." Not telling everyone everything that I do is a good thing too...like Dad used to say "God will remember" and that is all that matters.

I read on a Community Chat that a young man needed help for Christmas in 2021...he had no money or decorations and was pleading for help. I had Mom's little Christmas tree and didn't know what to do with it and got in my freezer and dug out meat and coffee and packed a whole bag of clothes for his wife.

I bought him and his 10 month old daughter clothes and had a whole pile of goodies in my parking lot for them to pick up. I made money on my house and gave them $100 cash. I called him and had him pick up the things and he was so grateful and excited and yelled to his wife "she gave us money!" He gave me a big hug, packed up his car with the goodies and took off. He was covered with tatoos but I try not to judge anyone for that. I felt so good I cried. He sent a picture of the tree all lit up and decorated...Mom felt good about that. I knew he had been working out at the church in Floyd so thought he was okay. As I got busier with Mom in Hospice I told the gals at the church to tell him I would not be responding for awhile. The night after Mom passed away I had the strongest sense of danger that I have ever felt...I went back into my bedroom and waited it out. I was reading the paper three nights after Mom passed and I read where this guy was booked on a $103,000 cash bond. He is facing two counts of first degree burglary, two counts of false imprisonment, two counts of tampering with a witness, and four counts of obstructing emergency communication. He had broke into an apartment and was accused of being armed with a box cutter and assaulting two male victims in their apartment leaving them with injuries. He allegedly threatened to stab the victims and kill them. He then went into another apartment with a gun and robbed them and threatened to kill them. I was sure that it must have been him that was lurking outside my place the night I felt that 'danger' feeling. When I told my dear friend Lance about it he said "Never have them come to your place!!" I learned a lesson big time and I was lucky it didn't turn out bad for me.

Our local young new priest came by and gave Mom last rites. They had a good visit and he was so sweet. When Mom first got bedridden, it was alot of work to keep her changed and clean and keep the bedding washed. My aunt and uncle came with their granddog Wilson and had a good visit with Mom. I continued on with the advice of my nurse friend I got through it. Finally things slowed down and Mom wasn't eating much and so I mostly had to change just wet desposable panties. I ordered her last meal from Pizza Ranch and they delivered it. She sat up in bed and thought it all tasted so good...chicken, mashed potatoes and gravy, macaroni salad, biscuits and I got a blueberry desert pizza..." mmmmm" was her response to everything. Once things slowed down my retired nurse friend via California told me to heat her blanket in the dryer, fluff her pillow, play relaxing music... make everything pleasant and comfortable for her. I was on it!! She loved the warm blankets and I played the Divine Mercy off of YouTube.com several times. My good friend and her husband had said the Divine Mercy and put a scapular around her neck. That was the same day that my friend called me into Mom's room and said "Look at that cardinal in that tree out there! It's been looking in here for an hour and hasn't moved at all!" I ran to my bedroom window and zoomed in on him and took his picture. I had that picture put on a canvas for them and myself. I know alot of people just say "oh that's just a bird! I don't know about that. Just a year ago at my house there was a cardinal that was under the arning and looking right at Mom in her recliner for quite awhile. I think it was Dad both times checking on Mom. Mom was so happy that my friends had prayed with her... it meant so much to her and she said it numerous times.

Hospice told me to expect Mom to see people and say things from the past amd just go along with it. She did. She woke up and asked "Why did that cow die?" and I knew she was back on the farm she was raised on. Another time she woke up and told me that she saw Lois & Ralph. I said "that is cool Mom".... they were the last friends of my folks to pass away. But the last thing that she said to me and I'll never forget it was "Oh...Dad is so handsome." I knew he was right there but I couldn't hear or see him and I wasn't hallucinating. I wasn't afraid instead it was so peaceful and comforting and sacred...I felt her folks and others were there too. It's like they had been in the next room. I had one foot in Heaven and one foot on Earth. That solidified my belief in Heaven and the hereafter. I wish my family could have witnessed that. The days after that people who wanted to say anything to Mom were welcome to call even though she couldn't answer...she could still hear and feel pain. My nephews had their kids talk and my cousin and Mom's sisters talked to her. I had gout in my left foot so bad due to the stress and having missed taking my gout pills when I went to the Tina Turner musical in New York. I could hardly turn Mom and welcomed friends that could help me at times. I used her walker to get around when it hurt bad. I complained to Hospice that they should not reduce their help during the holidays because people still die then. My retired nurse friend in California (aka Earth Angel) told me via phone to fluff Mom's pillow, warm her blanket and play some music. The last nights I played CDs and had a concert in Mom's room. She was starting to feel stiff and I would rub her down with coconut butter. I told her I loved her and thanked her for being the best mother anyone could have. I used a toothier to try to moisten Mom's lips but it took alittle skin off so I stopped. She was shutting down. I made a video in her room while she was laying there to the song 'Hero' by Mariah Carey ...I swear Jesus was helping me with that. It was Monday, January 3rd and when I woke up I could tell her breathing was very labored. A hospice pastor and our nun from our Catholic church stopped by to check on Mom and visit with each other. When I checked on Mom she had foam coming out of her mouth. The Hospice nurse came and ordered a pill to prevent that. I drove down to the pharmacy and got it and rushed back. I put the pill under Mom's tongue and she bit my finger!! It was because I was always having her close her mouth when I put the morphine in. I noticed that the pastor was still here. Another close friend of our family came by...she said she didn't want me to be alone. Sister D. left. Mom's Goddaughter from Dyersville had called earlier and was going to come the next day to spend the day with me. I didn't know for sure what was going on. I figured Mom had a couple days left.

The little Hospice aide that Mom liked so well sensed something and came at 2:30 pm instead of 4 pm like he had planned. When he went into the bedroom he whispered that he was there and Mom made a noise to acknowledge him. My friend and I heard Mom acknowledge him and we went out to the livingroom & he came out and his eyes were big and he said "Your Mom is active...I say she only has 1/2 hr to less than 2 hours to live." I looked over at my friend and asked her if I should call Mom's Goddaughter not to come. We decided to wait and see what happened first. We sat visiting and the aide came back out and said Mom had expired. It was 2:58 pm. I ran in and kissed Mom on her forehead. My friend and I were in shock. The aide told me that we had to call relatives and everyone important and then we would call the funeral home. I couldn't think real good but had some relatives call others to make it faster and easier on me. When all that was done the mortician came and the Hospice pastor was there to help him move Mom. They couldn't get the gurney around the corner to my second bedroom so the mortician wrapped her up in the flannel sheet and carried her out that way. We had to wait for a Hospice nurse to drive from St. Ansgar to officially pronounce her dead and dispense of all the medicine. Mom's birthday was January 17th and so was the nurse's from St. Angsgar. My friend that sat with me had a son killed 26 yrs ago in a motorcycle accident and his birthday was January 17th and he was my folk's Godson. I kidded that Mom and Dad would be at Betty White's 100th birthday in Heaven and that was on January 17th. My grandson had gone to Heaven on January 17th 2010. I talked to my dear friend that had said the Divine Mercy with Mom and she said that Mom had died at the brightest most sacred time to go to Heaven because Jesus died at 3 pm. It is written by Lady Fatima...you can google that and I believe it. Mom died on the 3rd of January at 3 pm and I had to meet the funeral director at 3 pm the next day. There were three of us with Mom when she passed. Another thing we noticed were the birds came to her birdfeeder in droves. Mom loved birds and evidently they loved her too.

Two really scary things happened while in the midst of taking Mom through Hospice. One day I was warming up some chicken, mashed potatoes and gravy and when I went to eat it I choked. My hiatal hernia seemed to cinch up and I couldn't breath. I threw up and got my breath back and I thought " Oh my dear Lord what if I would have died?!" Another time when I was all alone taking care of Mom I got the bug that was going around. I was sitting on the toilet with diahrrea and throwing up in a wastebasket on my lap. I thought "Dear Lord how can I care for my Mother like this?!" As fast as I got that bug it left me and I was ok to care for Mom. It is more ideal to have more that one person caring for a Hospice person but in my situation that wasn't an option.

This may sound weird but I was kind of on a high because the Hospice aide said that Mom had died without any pain. That was thanks to all the Hospice people coming over and telling me things at different stages. The one tip that I got was that a certain point you can't overdose them. You don't want them to go back to having pain because they can never get out of that pain and it is excruciating. I was diligent with administering morphine to keep Mom from feeling any pain. She still would grimace when she had to be turned or moved. It is true that they can hear and feel pain to the end. It was an amazing process to go through and I am glad I could do it for Mom but don't want to do it for anyone else if I can help it. I just wish my sons could have experienced some of this with me. My older nephews who stayed close to Mom and I wanted to come so bad but the weather was awful and the Covid was spiking again so Mom said that they shouldn't. They were with us to the end on the phone and wonderful support. I'll never forget the ones that helped us. Now it was time to write an obit. I think I wrote the best one ever but it helped that I was around so much and heard alot of stories about her life.

Mom's obit was as such: Marguerite "Jean" G. of Charles City passed away peacefully on Monday, January 3rd, 2022 at the age of 92 in her daughter's home: the love of her life came and took her home. Marguerite Jean (Loye) was the first born of three daughters to Marian (Howard) and Earl Loye on January 17, 1929 on a cold winter's day. Her father had to heat bricks to put on a horse drawn sleigh to bring her home. Jean was raised on the family farm on 250th Street in Charles City that her grandparents from Ireland had homesteaded until she was 14 years old. She moved in with some relatives in town so she could finish Junior and Senior High. She worked at a bakery and then at Sears. Dale had a friend call Jean to see if she would go out with him. Jean and her cousin Mary were noted as the "best looking brunettess" in town. That must have made Dale a little nervous. Jean knew who Dale's brother was and accepted and the rest is history. They got married on August 3rd, 1947 in Austin, MN at the Queen of Angels Catholic Church. They had four children. Jean worked at the ASCS Office, First Citizen's Bank, Breitbach Chiropractic and Saxony where she met many of her dearest lifelong friends. She loved her family and friends and was always there for them. One of her friends called her 'a little Irish lady who cooked in her kitchen and fed everybody'. When people were sending CARE packages to their kids in college back in the '70s, she was sending CARE packages to her sons in Vietnam. Jean was gifted to be able to "hand it over to God". Her faith was so strong. Jean and Dale loved to entertain friends and family. Dale would say "I'll clean the basement if you cook" to Mom and they would have a party. Jean and Dale loved to golf and go fishing on Minnesota lakes with family and friends. They also loved fishing on the Mississippi River. Jean was always there for everyone. I don't know how she did it but she rarely sat down in her younger years. She was never jealous or wasted time being envious of others. She gave, gave, gave to others and then gave some more. Jean was a 4H leader, St. Anthony Circle leader, volunteered to help at church functions and if there was a lemon pound cake on the kitchen counter, we had to ask if it was a 'funeral cake' or if we could eat it. Jean made everything she touched special whether it was food, a beautiful quilt or an embroidered piece she made. Jean loved to laugh and relished time spent with her grandchildren and great granddchildren, no matter if they lived near or far, she loved them all. Jean and Dale traveled and visited family wherever they lived until they couldn't. Jean was a special lady who lived simply, cared deeply, loved generously, spoke kindly and left the rest to God. She wanted donations in her name left to Immaculate Conception Elementary School, Messiah Food Pantry, Ronald McDonald House, St. Croix Hospice, Salvation Army, Wounded Warriors, Paralyzed Veterans and St. Jude's Children's Hospital.

Mom had decided on her own to be cremated and buried next to Dad. She also didn't want to have her service until the weather was better and relatives from the east coast could come. I picked June 25th because it was after my great niece's college graduation and it was also when my folk's best friend's son was going to be in town for his class reunion so that was when we buried Mom next to Dad in a private ceremony like she wanted. I spent time thinking about myself and what was next in my life. I had seen my Mom through Hospice practically alone. I had retired from a fantastic career and I needed to go on to my next chapter of my life. I know that the Good Lord will steer me the right way.

One thing I discovered during the Pandemic in 2020 was just how much fun it is to float on a lake on an inflatable float. My friend Barb and I would float for up to four hours at a time.

What we loved was the 'get away' from people and not having to wear a mask. It was totally therapeutic to us during that time and still is every summer.

I recently talked to JV and she had just seen her soulmate husband through Hospice after 46 years of a great marriage. She lives in Colorado. We still connect like we are never apart. I go to Tessie's Iowa Hawkeye tailgate parties every chance I get and dry to keep in touch with old friends as best I can. Tessie and her brother Tim and I hope to take in a Minnesota Vikings game this year...a bucket list for me.

I will probably think of other airline experiences that I have had after I close this book but have covered the majority of them. It is the most unique and adventurous career that you can ever experience and if you are interested in doing so, pursue it! Go online to several airlines and see what might work for you. Be sure that you love people and customer service and it is much easier if you live at a base and not have to commute.

I realized it is time to keep helping others...that's always a good way to help yourself feel better. I signed up to take online classes to sub for regular teachers. I got very attached to my 5th-8th grade study hall. I love to listen to them and was not the best at disciplining them. I told them right off the bat that I love them all and if I had my way they could have a party every day but it was a study hall so they had to keep it somewhat quiet. They would pour their guts out to me at times...it's not the same in this next generation's world. I had a stable home with parents that were never divorced and I never worried about having a meal. Alot of these kids don't have this and all they can do it is think about is fighting...not good. I talked to them about this more than their subjects. I strived to make them walk away from a fight rather to start one or partake in one. I also don't like how they are addicted to computer games and most games are about killing. Some girls dress too scimpy and there is nothing sacred about sex anymore which is alot of television's fault.

I talked to a friend who's mother needed help to stay in her home and decided to help her and I helped a Rotary friend during Ragbrai and volunteered at the KC serving food for the Ragbrai bunch. Ragbrai is a bike ride across Iowa that came through my hometown this year. I also was helping a friend with the NIACC (North Iowa Area Community College) Scholarship Fundraiser dinners. I had helped her for over 15 years and we only missed out on the 2020 dinner because of Covid. I am helping out a assisted living facility and absolutely love all the residents. Helping them, bringing them something home baked, listening to them and making them laugh makes me feel like I have purpose. I also decided to write a book about my life and career and hope if I make any money on my book and cooking show that I can spend it on my grandchildren who I love more than life itself. I thank my God, His Son and the Holy Spirit for all of my blessings and hope to do good unto others until the day I die.

Made in the USA
Coppell, TX
29 July 2024

35332905R00069